WHAT
LE

MW00478695

"Let me start by saying that if you are a leader, you need *Leadership Unleashed* by Todd Bishop as part of your library. It is not his first book, and it will not be his last, but it is his best so far. Every page is written with your success and achievement in mind. As you read it, you will discover why Todd Bishop is a leader of leaders."

Dr. Dave Martin, Best-Selling Author and Success Coach

"So many of us are trying to live and lead while being chained up. My friend and dynamic leader, Todd Bishop, has written an inspiring work that challenges us to doubt our doubts and feed our faith as we unleash our leadership. Get ready to experience the freedom of living out who you were meant to be!"

Pastor Ed Young, Lead Pastor, Fellowship Church, Dallas, Texas

"Whether you think you're a leader or not, YOU ARE; and my friend, Pastor Todd, has the book to help you lead well no matter what stage of life you're in. His ability to present practical leadership skills in an easy-to-read and applicable way is special. If you want to grow in your leadership knowledge, definitely start here!"

Travis Greene, Gospel Singer/Songwriter,
Lead Pastor, Forward City Church

"Leadership is not easy. It is full of challenges and difficulties that test our faith, trust and will." With these words, Todd Bishop unleashes 52 lessons on leadership which will expand your horizons, raise your expectations and answer vital questions. This is not just theory but tried-in-the-fire wisdom to help anyone desiring to please God as a leader."

Trevon Gross, PhD, Lead Pastor, Hope Cathedral, Jackson, NJ

"Todd is dynamic, creative and consistent. He lives what he teaches. I have personally grown as a leader walking with Todd! He is incredibly gifted as a communicator and leader. You will experience the life of an unleashed leader after reading Todd's latest book."

"Leadership starts with knowing the way and going the way. In his book, *Leadership Unleashed*, Pastor Todd does a fantastic job of also showing the way. He takes on the tough issues we all face with clear action steps that lead to resolution. It's also a great team study to help recognize, build and develop potential leaders in your organization. This is a must-read for anyone looking to take their leadership to the next level while developing a healthy team culture."

"Todd Bishop's mountainous leadership has planted him amongst the most successful and prominent leaders in our nation today. *Leadership Unleashed* literally unpacks a new dimension of wisdom for all leaders, both experienced and aspiring. Every leader who is yearning for unique distilled knowledge needs to read this book!"

"Todd Bishop is one of the most passionate and intentional leaders I've had the pleasure of meeting. He is the definition of what the Bible calls a "shepherd." He does all he can to lead and care for the people God has entrusted him with in a way that is nothing short of excellent and honoring to God. If you want to unlock your leadership potential—and for God to unleash His purpose in your life—read this book!"

"Leadership is a subject that is often easier to talk about than it is to be about. Todd Bishop is a rare example of the opposite. He is one of the greatest teachers I have ever met, but he is even better in person than through a screen or a book. If you are looking to learn from someone who is actually DOING it, and doing it the right way, *Leadership Unleashed* will bless you."

"I couldn't recommend *Leadership Unleashed* enough! I have known Todd for over a decade and have seen firsthand the impact of his leadership wisdom. A person's leadership mettle is revealed during challenging times, and Todd showed this during the COVID crisis. Unlike many churches who experienced drop off and setback, Church Unleashed nearly doubled in size. Some may think this was coincidental, but those who know understand that it is the result of great leadership. In this book, Todd shares some of his leadership nuggets with you. You will become a better leader."

Frank Santora, Lead Pastor, Faith Church,
New Milford, CT, www.faithchurch.cc

"Great leadership can move us. Great leaders can ignite passions and inspire greatness. Todd Bishop's *Leadership Unleashed*, is a compilation of 52 leadership lessons from a man truly deep in his faith. It helps identify one's personal leadership potential for making positive impacts on others' lives. I personally welcome God back in the workplace!

Organized in an orderly 52 lessons on achieving requirements for true leadership and propelling personal improvement, the book gives an interesting, real-world, real-experience, practical approach to working towards true leadership, personal freedom and goal fulfillment. The lessons contain real, relatable personal stories, examples and events from Todd Bishop's and experiences with family, his congregation and the Church. He is a pastor for and leads Church Unleashed. Todd humbly states, "There is no way a single book can inspire your leadership, not even this one, except for the Bible. I believe the Bible is the greatest leadership book that has ever been written." I thoroughly enjoyed this book and its real-world, practical lessons taught from personal experiences in the light of God, the Bible and the Church.

I highly recommend this book for people who lead—or who aspire to lead—through personal growth and positive impact. A motivational must-read . . . and as Pastor Todd states, "Great leaders emerge from great learnings!" It is my opinion that we need more teachers and leaders that have their fundamentals centered around our Lord and Savior Jesus Christ, and who exercise the Holy Word in the workplace, the home and the church on Sundays!

I thank you for the opportunity to express my feelings and my gratitude for reviewing Todd's journey and the life lessons I have learned."

Dominick Sartorio, Executive Chairman, Vantage Health, LLC, Vantagehealth.com

"Looking for an amazing resource to train, encourage and fire up your team? Then you have found the right resource in *Leadership Unleashed*! Todd Bishop gives us a book not based on theory but on everyday, practical ministry life! *Leadership Unleashed* is raw, honest and full of great stories that Todd and his team have walked through for years building a great church in Long Island and impacting an entire region!"

Anthony Milas, Granite United Church

"Relationship building is an ongoing process in ministry. When we attend events like conferences, lunches and meetings, we always leave having made new connections. True, lifelong friends are few and far between. My friendship with Todd and Mary spans over two decades. He has always pushed the envelope in areas of creativity and is a leader among leaders. His love and drive for the local church is refreshing. If you're a pastor or other leader who wants to better yourself and your team, you'll find a wealth of useful information in this book. Instantly, the short chapters and questions will be just what you need for upcoming staff meetings and coaching sessions. Without question a recommended read!"

Steve Bellavia, Lead Pastor, Relate Church, Virginia Beach, VA

"Leadership is hard. That's why I believe God places the sharpest tools in the hardest soil. Todd Bishop is no exception to that rule. In *Leadership Unleashed*, Todd serves up proven leadership axioms in easy-to-digest doses that will unleash the leader inside of you. The leadership wisdom in this book, born out of decades of in-the-trenches work, is leadership gold."

David Crosby, Lead Pastor, Community Church, Pocono, Pennsylvania

"Todd Bishop has empowered many to face life with a mindset that says, "I am in complete control of my personal growth." My time spent beside him has created opportunities for me to grow into a subservient leader for my team. He has also allowed players to realize true leadership within the framework of TEAM. I will keep this book close by! Forever grateful."

Bryan Collins, Former Head Football Coach - Long Island University (8 Championships), Defensive Line Coach - Stonybrook University, Long Island, New York

"I've personally worked alongside several of the most influential leaders in the world and have discovered that truly impactful leadership advice can be a rare find. *Leadership Unleashed* offers a perspective many don't, and tackles everything from achieving world-class standards to creating a legacy of which you can be proud. If you are an owner or CEO—if you are in any form of leadership—I am convinced this book will transform the way you lead."

Jennifer Figueroa, President, 1Network Company, Garden City, NY

"This book, *Leadership Unleashed*, professionally, practically, and profoundly addresses the internal drive in every one of us to be better leaders in all areas of life! It brilliantly and creatively provides ways to succeed. What we lack in motivation and resources is provided for us in this great book. It is a must-read! Author Todd Bishop is a proven, effective leader in his home, church, community and cherished friendships, which are all attributed to his commitment and determination to be the very best at what he does and who he is!"

Gary Bruegman, Counselor/Therapist, Former Dean of Students—CBC Denver, Colorado

"The applications are limitless when it comes to Pastor Todd Bishop's newest book, *Leadership Unleashed*. I've not read anything else this comprehensive yet this simple. I promise you that *Leadership Unleashed* will never make it to your bookshelf. Why not? Because it will be on your desk for years to come. You'll use this book for the rest of your life as a leader."

Scott Hagan, Ph.D., President, North Central University

Unless otherwise marked, all Scripture quotations are taken from the Holy Bible, New Living Translation, copyright © 1996, 2004, 2015 by Tyndale House Foundation. Used by permission of Tyndale House Publishers, Inc., Carol Stream, Illinois 60188. All rights reserved. | Scripture quotations marked KJV are taken from the King James Version of the Bible. Public domain. | Scripture quotations marked NIV are taken from the Holy Bible, New International Version®, NIV®. Copyright © 1973, 1978, 1984, 2011 by Biblica, Inc.™ Used by permission of Zondervan. All rights reserved worldwide. www.zondervan.com. The "NIV" and "New International Version" are trademarks registered in the United States Patent and Trademark Office by Biblica, Inc.™

For foreign and subsidiary rights, contact the author.

Cover design by: Sara Young
Cover photo by: Billion Photos

ISBN: 978-1-959095-73-6   1 2 3 4 5 6 7 8 9 10

Printed in the United States of America

TAKE YOUR LIFE
TO ANOTHER LEVEL

LEADERSHIP
UNLEASHED

TODD R. BISHOP

DEDICATION

I am grateful for my amazing bride, Mary, and the incredible three gifts our love has produced—Malachi, Abigayl, & Bethany. Thank you for all the sacrifices you make—seen and unseen. I am better because of you!

To the most incredible staff at Church Unleashed, thank you for being such an easy team to love and lead. You have been my greatest experiment of leadership and you all have made me so proud. Keep unleashing your leadership! You are just getting started!

ACKNOWLEDGMENTS

Success rarely belongs to the individual. Gina Bellomo, Malachi Bishop, Olivia Diaz, & Amya Mitchell, I could not have done this without y'all. This Creative Team at CHURCH UNLEASHED invested hours, passion, and excellence in helping me complete *Leadership Unleashed*. You are more than part of my team, you are family. I would also like to thank the team at AVAIL PUBLISHING for believing in this project and making their entire team available from start to finish in order to make *Leadership Unleashed* come to life. I am so grateful.

CONTENTS

FOREWORD

Can I tell you just a little about my friend, Todd Bishop? He's weird! Yes, it's true. Todd just has this peculiar fire that burns inside of him for the heart of God and His people. He can't just pastor a nice little flock in the middle of the Bible Belt. Heck nooooooo! He and his wife, Mary, have built something that few people have ever been able to accomplish—a STRONG, vibrant church smack dab in the middle of Long Island! (Talk about your tough crowds!) But that hasn't slowed him down. Pastor Todd is bold, relevant, funny, invested, and incredibly smart! (He made me write that . . . just kidding!) He is ON FIRE! He's leading the church and unleashing the power, favor, and grace of God on an entire region . . . and now with *Leadership Unleashed* . . . on the whole WORLD!

I have to be honest. This will probably not be like any other leadership book you've read. It contains no grand unusable theories. This is a seriously high-octane life manual. Jam-packed! Clear. Concise. Not a wasted word. Cleverly precise, Todd has laid out fifty-two amazing leadership lessons that

FOREWORD

he painstakingly collected over the years. In fact, he's done all the work FOR us and given us one, easy-to-digest lesson for each week of our leadership year. How convenient is that? Sorry—no leadership mumbo jumbo here. Just a relevant, readable, entertaining primer of basic truths for any staff person or leader—a wonderful resource for your corporate or ministry teams.

Leadership Unleashed is going to light a fresh fire under your business or church and help you keep your purpose alive! This will be your new go-to guide for teams. (I'm already thinking of people I need to give this book to.) I especially love that Pastor Todd reminds us that our potential, our passion, and our purpose are often mesmerizing to others and critical for our success. So, don't hide that fire or EVER apologize for it. Like moths to a flame, if you have FIRE within you, people will always be drawn to watch it burn! Don't shy away from the spark that God has ignited in you. Exploit it. Bask in its warmth and light.

Fan your flame, UNLEASH the power of God's favor on your purpose, and watch it spread like wildfire!

Blessings!
Nicole Crank
Host of the international TV program
The Nicole Crank Show, best-selling
author, conference speaker, senior
co-pastor of FaithChurch.com

INTRODUCTION

I started my leadership journey in 1991 at Central Bible College in Springfield, Missouri. So, that is a whole lot of years of learning and leading that I have had the privilege of experimenting in! Yes, it has been a lifelong leadership experiment. As I have had the privilege of leading people, groups, leaders, and organizations, I have discovered many things about myself. Success and failure are equally great teachers.

Every person is a leader! It's true! Everybody leads something. The real question is, "What kind of leader do you want to be?" This was something I had to wrestle with in the early years on my path of leadership. I made a lot of mistakes (and I still do), but I am grateful that God has allowed me to be part of this experiment called leadership. I have not arrived! To be honest, I even hesitate to write this resource because there are so many more gifted, talented leaders out there. Or maybe that is just my insecurity screaming in my head! Despite these thoughts and feelings, I was on a plane traveling to West Palm Beach, and I felt God tell me to write this book: *Leadership*

Unleashed. Six months later, it was finished. Full circle. So here it goes! This is more than a book to me. It is a calling!

Over the last three decades of leadership, I have watched leaders come and go from every sphere of life. Many finished well; others were finished. Somewhere along the way, we either lose our edge, or we sharpen it. The key to lasting in leadership is sharpening your edge.

Ecclesiastes 10:10 reads, "Using a dull ax requires great strength, so sharpen the blade." I believe that *Leadership Unleashed is an opportunity for you to sharpen your blade* . . . to drill down deep into your leading and raise your lid.

Great leaders emerge from great learning! I have put together fifty-two leadership lessons that have helped me become a better leader. *Leadership Unleashed is designed to be a simple read with* insightful principles that will elevate you and expand your potential over the course of one year. Many of these lessons I learned from others, adapted them to various situations, and made my own. Regardless, they will have a profound impact on your life and leadership.

My prayer is that you would experience *LEADERSHIP UNLEASHED* in your life, marriage, family, church, business, nonprofit, sports team, or start-up! So, as you dive into this book, get active: mark it up, write notes, ask questions, reflect, and tear into it!

Unleash the leader inside of you!

NEVER ASK ANYONE TO DO WHAT YOU ARE UNWILLING TO DO

"**N**ever ask anyone to do what you are unwilling to do." This is one of the most important ministry mantras I have put into practice over the last three decades of my leadership journey. Why? It matters! Setting the example sets the tone for any organization.

> *"Never ask anyone to do what you are unwilling to do."*

Too many leaders tell someone to pick up the trash in the hallway when they—themselves—won't even make an attempt. I have often told our team, "I will never ask you to do anything I will not do or have not done." It is a slogan that is said in and around our offices a lot.

You see, if serving is beneath us, then leadership is beyond us. Nothing should be beneath us. Leaders must be willing to do anything they ask their team to do. Notice that I did not say they are *supposed* to do it, but they must be willing. It's a posture of the heart. If we are unwilling to do it, then we should not ask anyone else to do it either.

When a group sees their team leader setting the bar high by being a great example, it motivates them. It is inhibitive to the success of any business, nonprofit, or church for leaders to avoid doing something because it is "beneath" them.

One of the most inspiring traits of a great leader is humility. This principle is all about being humble. Employers, entrepreneurs, and even pastors will become their own lid if they lead with pride. The one who can reach down to pick up the piece of paper off the floor is now qualified to lead a Fortune 500 company. Don't limit the power of humility.

A lot of people like to tell other people what to do. Honestly, there are times when I like it too! However, the real test of leadership is not just telling someone what to do; it's showing them how to do it. Setting an example of servanthood and sacrifice is a must for every leader.

The easiest leaders to follow are the ones who are serving in the trenches with you. If you look over your life, you will quickly discover that the employers you enjoyed working for the most were the ones who didn't just know the way; they showed you the way.

Now, as leaders, we cannot do everything. Notice the principle: never ask anyone to do what you are unwilling to do! At some point in your leadership, you will not be able—for whatever reason—to do the things you did when you first started. As your business, church, or nonprofit grows, the less you will be able to do, but you must always be willing to do it!

When my wife and I first started our church, we did everything. Our church was portable, so we had to set up and tear down before and after our services. Mary would run the kids' ministry, and I would run the adult services. Everything fell to us—even the follow-up on every first-time guest. In the beginning, it was challenging, but we never complained about it. We just did it.

NEVER ASK ANYONE TO DO WHAT YOU ARE UNWILLING TO DO

When leaders complain about what they are doing, they are revealing their unwillingness to do the mundane. I learned many years ago: if we are unwilling to do the mundane, then we will be unable to do the magnificent. As leaders, we must set the example by never asking anyone to do what we are or were unwilling to do.

So, let's get out in the trenches and lead by example!

UNLEASH YOUR THOUGHTS

Where have you allowed pride to keep you from doing something you felt was beneath you?

_____

_____

_____

_____

_____

_____

_____

_____

_____

What are some ways that you can show those you lead that you are willing to serve alongside them?

_____

_____

_____

_____

_____

_____

_____

_____

_____

To become a better example to those you lead, what might you need to change?

_____

_____

_____

_____

_____

_____

_____

_____

What are some things you should stop doing that you have been willing to do?

_____

_____

_____

_____

_____

_____

_____

_____

_____

_____

_____

EVERY MOMENT MATTERS

Our goal has to be to use every moment, every minute, every second, and every breath for what matters most! Here's what I know: we don't want to live our entire lives working for the wrong things! We need to find what God designed us for and then give 125 percent of our energy to that thing that matters most.

The Bible declares, "Seek the Kingdom of God above all else, and live righteously, and he will give you everything you need" (Matthew 6:33). This is about priorities. In fact, the whole Bible is about priorities. It truly teaches that every moment matters.

One of the worst things, IMO (that means "in my opinion"), is to get to the end of your life and say, "I should have . . ." or, "I could have . . ." or, "I would have. . . ." At some point, we are all going to die! Amen, that's good news. Let's pray. You can stop reading now! Kidding—but the fact is that a person's life must have higher value than a checklist or their pocketbook.

When we get to the end of our lives, we will have to ask, *What did I spend my life doing?* We don't want to get stuck having to say the following:

- "I would have started that business, but. . . ."
- "I should have written that novel, but. . . ."
- "I could have done so much more if only. . . ."

The challenge—today—is that you don't want to waste your life doing the earthly at the expense of the eternal. In other words, what is most important? Whatever that is should be the center of our focus. Every moment matters!

I was invited to attend a conference that I did not want to attend, but I wrestled with going simply out of loyalty. I went back and forth, thinking about it for a few weeks. Finally, I called a friend for some advice.

He asked me one question: "Would you recommend this conference to a friend?"

My immediate answer was, "No way."

He responded, "Then why would you waste your time attending something you would not recommend?"

Here's why this matters: if I had attended, I would have been wasting my time at a conference I did not want to attend, thinking I could be putting my efforts into something with greater influence.

Every moment. Every minute. Every second. Every breath. Did you know that the average person takes approximately twenty thousand breaths each day?[1] That's about 575 million breaths in a lifetime. Every single one matters.

As leaders, our priority has to be to use every moment for what matters most. Priorities change based on what is needed in the moment. That's why it is critical to use every conscious opportunity to do the things that will create the biggest impact on people's lives. A business is not just a business—it is an opportunity to change someone's life! The iPhone changed people's lifestyles and habits. However, that little phone can keep you on social media instead of socializing. That single

---

1 "How Many Breaths You Take per Day & Why It Matters," *ADVENT Knows*, 4 May 2021, https://adventknows.com/blog/how-many-breaths-you-take-per-day-why-it-matters/.

piece of technology can keep you from using your every breath to make the greatest impact on people.

> *Use every moment you have, while you have it, to do what you have been called to do.*

Don't waste your life on things that do not matter! Use every moment you have, while you have it, to do what you have been called to do. And don't be distracted by someone else's priorities. Your life will head in the direction of your priorities!

UNLEASH YOUR THOUGHTS

In what areas have you allowed others to determine your priorities?

_____

_____

_____

_____

_____

_____

_____

_____

_____

When do you find it hard to say no to the good, so you can say yes to the best?

_____

_____

_____

_____

_____

_____

_____

_____

_____

What is your greatest struggle in writing your goals?

_____

_____

_____

_____

_____

_____

_____

_____

_____

_____

Write down your greatest distractions. Create a plan of action to reduce their effects on your daily habits.

_____

_____

_____

_____

_____

_____

_____

_____

_____

_____

OWN YOUR FLAWS

OWN YOUR FLAWS

O wning one's flaws is a huge but often overlooked leadership trait. Most people lift up their strengths and ignore their flaws. However, I believe one of the most important things we can do as leaders is to own our flaws. It's never easy, but it is essential if we want to connect with our teams and the rest of the people we lead.

I was preparing a teaching for an all-staff meeting, and I needed my personal assistant to take care of one of the tasks associated with it. That task did not get done. I stated publicly, "I need a new PA." That being said, I carried on, but before I finished the meeting, I felt the need to apologize—publicly. I owned it.

I wish I could say I own it all the time. I try really hard to, but it's tough for me. This is a tough thing for a lot of leaders. However, this may be one of the most important habits we ever develop. As Craig Groeschel, leadership guru, always says in his podcast, "People would rather follow a leader who is always real rather than a leader who is always right." Real leaders own their flaws.

As a pastor, I find myself always talking about my issues in my sermons. It is kind of therapeutic. It humanizes me. I grew up in a church culture where the pastor made his followers feel like he had reached a state of holiness higher than they could ever hope to attain. It was a turn-off for me. When I went into ministry, I made a decision that I was going to own my flaws and just be me.

Now, this does not mean I reveal all of my deepest, darkest secrets. A leader can't share those things with everyone. But every leader makes mistakes. There is no way around it. And leaders typically make their mistakes publicly. That's part of the harsh reality of leadership: our mistakes are not just *our* mistakes! That's why you have to own your flaws ASAP.

"I don't want to make mistakes," you say.

Absolutely, I agree! Mistakes are not our mission, but they are part of the process. All people make mistakes, but married people find out about theirs sooner! But it's not just our spouse who sees and possibly points out our mistakes. Our team sees them, so we are better off owning them than ignoring them. If we ignore our flaws, we will lose our credibility, but when we own them, our leadership gains credibility.

The Bible declares, "If we claim we have no sin, we are only fooling ourselves and not living in the truth" (1 John 1:8). Nobody is perfect—we are going to make mistakes. But our mistakes don't have to make us! Read that again. You are not what you have done but what Jesus has done for you. Mistakes just prove you are trying!

> *I learned this principle years ago: "Your best teacher is your last mistake!"*

I learned this principle years ago: "Your best teacher is your last mistake!" We don't have to obsess over our mistakes or flaws. No, we learn from them and move on. However, if we never own them, we will never learn from them. If we never learn, we will never grow! While this is one of the parts of personal or corporate growth that leaders don't enjoy, it is an irreplaceable gift to your organization that will have immediate and long-term benefits.

Own your flaws! Deal with private mistakes differently, though. Private issues don't have to be public mentions. Be careful where you share your private challenges; own those under the accountability of a trusted few. But the public ones . . . own them!

UNLEASH YOUR THOUGHTS

Why are you afraid of owning your flaws—especially when everyone sees the public ones?

_____

_____

_____

_____

_____

_____

_____

_____

_____

_____

What flaws have been brought to your attention that you have not owned? Why haven't you owned them?

_____

_____

_____

_____

_____

_____

_____

_____

_____

Is there someone you need to apologize to publicly for something you said or did to them publicly?

_____

_____

_____

_____

_____

_____

_____

_____

_____

_____

Do you need some counseling or extra help with some inner conflict?

_____

_____

_____

_____

_____

_____

_____

_____

_____

_____

LANGUAGE MATTERS

This is a leadership mantra I shout to our staff all the time. Hear me today, leader: language matters! In every email, text, conversation, public message, or video broadcast, your language matters!

In every email, text, conversation, public message, or video broadcast, your language matters!

In the communication arena, we need to be like the language police. If we hear someone misspeak, we need to catch it and correct it. Don't wait. Catch it. Correct it. That seems crazy. Yes, I am crazy about language. Why? It matters!

I often catch our staff saying something a little different than the way I said it. When that happens, I say, "That's not right. It's this." I'll state what I said and then remind them, "Language matters." You see, great teammates don't craft their own language. They echo the language of their leader.

The church I lead has a vision. It is pretty simple. "We exist to inspire hope, unleash potential, and change lives." I once had a staff member list those tenets in the wrong order. I immediately stopped and said, "Language matters." We have to put those goals in the right order because there is a process to our mission.

You may be thinking, *You seem crazy about language.* Yep, you are right. I am always working toward making sure our language honors our mission. There is no option when it comes to all of us sharing that same language. It makes it easier for people to grasp it and more difficult for hijackers to dilute it.

Our words have the power of life or death in them! I am always going to try and choose words that offer the following:

- HOPE
- LIFE
- ENCOURAGEMENT

That's my default setting. But, to be honest, sometimes my words don't come out right.

King David understood imperfection, failure, and poor choices. That is why he wrote this prayer: "May the words of my mouth and the meditation of my heart be pleasing to you, O LORD, my rock and my redeemer" (Psalm 19:14). David understood the power of words. Language matters! It is vital to the success of any organization, business, or church. If you want your leadership unleashed, then you, as a leader, must drill down into your language. It affects everything around you.

The way leaders communicate must be different! Oh, man, the world needs to hear this today! A leader can't have a negative mouth and live a positive life. I choose to be positive and encouraging, just like the Christian radio station K-Love! Your whole team must learn to echo and copy your heart and words. If they are not able to do this, confusion will reign in your organization.

LANGUAGE MATTERS

Another hazard of not being focused on your organization's corporate language is that someone will start a new language. That will not only result in confusion, but it could also lead to division. Here's my advice on messaging:

- Choose clear over clever—every time.
- Choose clear over creative—every time.

Not everyone "gets" clever, so that opportunity is wasted. Some people try to get creative, and the message gets lost in the creativity. That's why language matters!

The most successful leaders in human history taught their followers to echo their message. Be that kind of leader, and watch your leadership get unleashed!

UNLEASH YOUR THOUGHTS

Where have there been language issues with you as a leader?

_____

_____

_____

_____

_____

_____

_____

_____

_____

_____

_____

What can you do to change your language?

_____

_____

_____

_____

_____

_____

_____

_____

_____

_____

Whom can you talk to if you need a vocabulary coach?

_____

_____

_____

_____

_____

_____

_____

_____

_____

_____

_____

LEADERS DON'T JUST GO TO THE NEXT LEVEL, THEY GROW TO THE NEXT LEVEL

"Leaders don't just go to the next level. They *grow* to the next level." Real leadership is all about growth. To be clear, growth is not always numerical. How it's measured is determined by the area in which the growth happens. It could be the broadening of vision, multiplication of finances, deepening of character, or expansion of staff or team—the opportunities for growth are endless. The challenge is that most leaders measure growth in one way: numbers.

When Mary and I started our church in 2008, we did not experience numerical growth instantly. Ours was a sluggish beginning. I remember calling a pastor-friend when we finally reached one hundred people on a Sunday. It was about three years into our church plant, and I was celebrating! His response was disheartening, to say the least, "Well, Todd, I wish you had gotten here sooner." Are you kidding me? Seriously!

What this pastor failed to see was the growth that was happening in my wife and me. We needed to grow personally before we could grow as a church. People don't see that until much later. Sadly, that pastor's comment wrecked me and that relationship. He was only looking at numbers—he did not see our development as leaders.

Leaders don't just go to the next level. They grow to the next level! And God had to do some work in us before He could work through us. Here's what you have to understand: YOU need to grow before your business, church, or nonprofit can grow! It all starts with you. Let me ask you a question,

"How are you growing—not in what you do but in who you are? Only great leaders will master this lesson.

> *How do you grow? That has to be the $40-million question because it's different for everybody.*

How do you grow? That has to be the $40-million question because it's different for everybody. I heard someone say many years ago, "Leaders are readers." While that may be true for some, not everyone learns through the pages of a book. I like to say it this way, "Leaders are learners." I don't care how I learn or how someone else learns. Our concern as leaders should never be how we learn but that we learn.

Therefore, the best thing you can do for yourself is to figure out your most effective method of learning. How you learn will determine how you grow! Once you've determined your growth mechanism,—what causes you to think deeper or more creatively, nothing will stunt you.

Many leadership gurus will tell you how you can grow. What they are actually telling you is how they grew. In fact, we should be more descriptive than prescriptive in our mentoring and coaching relationships. I may find growth through podcasts, but you may find it in *Forbes* magazine. And don't ever get locked into one method because as you grow, you'll find yourself changing. How you grew at twenty will be different than how you grow at forty. None of us are the same as we were even ten years ago. Keep growing. Keep going. Never look back, and trust God with your progress!

Learn. Grow. Develop. Repeat. Learn. Grow. Develop. Repeat.

That is the healthy rhythm of a leader. We cannot hit the pause button on personal growth. It is a dynamic that needs to be nurtured and developed for the rest of our lives. Keep learning. Keep growing. Keep developing. Then repeat that pattern again.

Let me add this caveat regarding growth mechanisms. There are certain ones that every leader can learn from or through. The first is motivation. If you can decide what motivates you, it will be easier to grow. We lean into what gives us purpose and meaning. A stay-at-home parent may be motivated to also be a homeschool parent. A CEO may be motivated by personal success. An entrepreneur may be motivated to create a global brand. Your motivation is what drives you, and it is a strong factor in speeding up growth.

Second, we have to embrace being critiqued. This is one of the most difficult steps. Those around you are near you because they believe in you. They are bound to critique you. What is critique? It is when someone tells you something you need to hear to make you better. It's different than being critical. Criticism usually comes from people who think they are better. It feels condescending, and there's a huge difference. Embrace critique.

Third, you have to learn from those with more experience than you. Surround yourself with leaders who are beyond where you are. This is vital. You will then avoid many of the pitfalls they have experienced and get to your success goals quicker—all because you put the right people in your learning environment.

Finally, invest in yourself. Yes, spend time and money on you. Grow your leadership. Here's the reality: no one should care more about your leadership than you. Invest in yourself.

UNLEASH YOUR THOUGHTS

Growth doesn't just happen numerically. What are some ways that God is currently stretching and growing you?

_____

_____

_____

_____

_____

_____

_____

_____

_____

_____

How can you keep consistently growing in this area?

_____

_____

_____

_____

_____

_____

_____

_____

_____

What is your habit of learning? What habits of learning can you put into action right now?

_____

_____

_____

_____

_____

_____

_____

_____

_____

_____

_____

_____

WHAT YOU BUILD YOU MUST MAINTAIN

L eaders are builders. Some build something out of nothing; those are the creative entrepreneurs. Others build on top of something; those are the innovative entrepreneurs. We need both types of builders. No matter how someone builds, they have something in common: they must maintain what they have built.

> *No matter how someone builds, they have something in common: they must maintain what they have built.*

The first building our church purchased in 2011 was a 6,000-square-foot storefront. It was a very small building. Everything was inexpensive. Then, in 2015, we purchased a 30,000-square-foot building, and our costs went through the roof. It was an eye-opening experience for Mary and me. The same is true in your business, church, or nonprofit.

In 2021, Mary and I were able to purchase a larger house, twice the size of our prior house. According to the bank, we could afford it because our debt-to-income ratio was perfect. Here's the thing: the bank does not take into account that the cost of utilities will triple and lawn care will double, and the maintenance will be more complex. Yes, we bought a bigger house, but that house came with bigger bills and bigger responsibilities.

The same is going to be true for you. Whether you are building your business or buying a bigger home, there will be greater costs. The Bible declares, "But don't begin until you count the cost. For who would begin construction of a building without first calculating the cost to see if there is enough money to finish it?" (Luke 14:28). What you build, you must maintain.

It does not matter what you are building. Whatever it is, you truly have to count the cost of not just building it but maintaining it. That is going to require something called, um, work! That's part of the maintaining process. Many people crave the success, but they don't realize the cost of that success.

Bigger buildings. Bigger dreams. Bigger budgets. All of those require a building and a maintenance mindset. You need both. I have heard many leaders over the years say, "Don't get stuck in maintenance mode." But there is a level of need for maintenance. Each time you board a plane, I am sure you are grateful they did some routine maintenance to keep you and the rest of the passengers safe. Building is vital, but maintaining is equally as critical to success.

Never forget that when you build something, you are responsible for maintaining it. A bigger parking lot requires a higher cost of maintenance. A larger family requires a bigger budget for food, utilities, and housing. There is no way around the need for a building and a maintenance mindset.

Now, let me say this; you cannot live in maintenance mode, but you need it. Our drive as leaders needs to always be focused on the future. That's a fact. But you cannot neglect care at the expense of calling. That's why you have to under-stand what you build, you must maintain.

Building is only the beginning. Maintaining takes planning, hard work, and diligence. No matter what God calls you to build, make sure you are putting in the effort to maintain the calling of God on your life and leadership.

UNLEASH YOUR THOUGHTS

Have you honestly counted the cost of what you are building?

_____

_____

_____

_____

_____

_____

_____

_____

_____

_____

What areas need more attention to maintenance?

_____

_____

_____

_____

_____

_____

_____

_____

_____

WHAT YOU BUILD YOU MUST MAINTAIN

What can you do now to course correct, so you can keep consistently building?

_____

_____

_____

_____

_____

_____

_____

_____

_____

_____

_____

_____

_____

_____

_____

_____

YOU CAN'T BE BIASED AGAINST YOUR FAMILY

have a confession to make: I believe in nepotism. In fact, I believe it is a biblical model of development. Now, I do not believe in promoting the unqualified. But the fact is, I am never going to be biased against my family. In other words, I can't discount my wife and children because they have the last name Bishop.

My wife and I started our church on our own. Yes, we enlisted financial support and partners, but the reality remains that it was 100 percent on us. We have worked the ground ever since, and we have done this together! Not just us—our kids have sacrificed so much for the kingdom of God with many late nights and long days of working, serving, giving, helping, blessing, and sacrificing.

As I have examined Scripture, I can easily see that God worked in people and often through families! That's why Matthew wrote the genealogy of Jesus to reveal His kingly lineage. God also chose His Son to carry on the work of salvation for the nations! Whom did God choose? His Son. You see, as a leader, you can't be biased against your family. Now, that does not mean you have to hire them or work with them, but you cannot *not* hire them because they are related to you.

Now, working with family has its challenges. That's a fact, Jack! It is one of the most rewarding things in life, but it is also filled with many opportunities for grace!

I have the great honor and privilege of working alongside my wife. She is a gifted leader, communicator, and pastor. But above all that, she loves Jesus, is an incredible spouse, and is an amazing mother. I know her focus is God's house, but we start building God's house in our house! That's why I believe our kids want to go to church, and not just go to church, but serve in the church. Building the church is not just a Mom and Dad thing; it is a family thing!

> *Building the church is not just a Mom and Dad thing; it is a family thing!*

My oldest, Malachi, works at the church, but he also works on the church. He has wisdom beyond his years. He knows the history of our church better than anyone else. He has the heart of the house because he has the heart of his father and mother. We never forced it, but we encouraged it. Mary and I are so humbled by the man he is becoming. So, yes, I will never be biased against my family.

Refuse to allow the culture we live in to redefine how you lead what you lead. Obviously, you must do it with integrity and character, but honor your family by giving them opportunities. Most priests and kings of the Bible came from a family line of priests and kings. Many screwed up, but many more excelled in their calling.

I know for me, my family will always have a seat at the table where I lead, whether it's my church, my nonprofit, or my LLC. When I say you should do life with your family, that's not just vacations! It's about doing life together, and if you have the privilege of hiring family, and they are called to do what you need, don't overlook them because of their last name.

I believe in nepotism because I believe it's a biblical model.

UNLEASH YOUR THOUGHTS

Have you included your family in your ministry/leadership? If so, how?

_____

_____

_____

_____

_____

_____

_____

_____

_____

_____

What has been the result of including your family?

_____

_____

_____

_____

_____

_____

_____

_____

_____

_____

_____

Do you believe in biblical nepotism? Why/why not?

_____

_____

_____

_____

_____

_____

_____

_____

_____

_____

If you have allowed culture to redefine your leadership, what are some steps you can take to counter that?

_____

_____

_____

_____

_____

_____

_____

_____

_____

_____

SUCK IT UP, CUPCAKE

I believe that we have developed a culture of people who can't take a joke, any criticism, or an insult. All of those things are part of leadership. Pastor Paul Bartholomew, a great man I had the honor of serving alongside, once said, "A leader cannot have a glass jaw because sometimes you have to take it on the chin." That is so freakin' true.

If you really want to unleash your leadership, there are going to be times when you have to just "suck it up." Not everything is going to go your way. To be honest, most things are going to take twists and turns you do not expect. Often, you just have to put your shoulders back, stick out your chest, and push through what life has brought you to.

I have experienced several opportunities to "suck it up" in my nearly three decades of leadership. I have had to apologize for what I did not do. There were moments when I took potshots from people who were supposed to be friends. At the end of the day, one of the greatest tests of leadership is the ability to take some hits.

I have several friends who, at the first sign of difficulty, run in the opposite direction. They cave in. They quit. But remember, leadership is not a sprint. It is a marathon. It is not always about who is the fastest. Many times it is more about who is faithful. In fact, too many leaders choose flight over fight. But as a lifelong New Yorker, I am going to slug it out until there is no breath left in me. I am going to suck it up and keep swinging.

Leaders will face seasons when they just have to put on their "big person pants" and do what needs to be done. Haters are gonna hate. That's why we have to keep pushing forward—beyond the difficulty, beyond the pain—to do what God has called us to do in life and leadership.

Criticism is just part of the leadership journey. We are all going to face it more than we want to. Some of that criticism is going to really sting or hurt deeply. When it comes to critical words spoken to you or about you, it is imperative to look within to see if there is a shade of truth in them. Sometimes the criticism hurts so much because you know it is somewhat true. Despite the criticism, we must "suck it up."

There will be people on every side of you that are trying to pull you down. Rise higher. Stand stronger. Expand your belief. God has more before you than hell has behind you! Keep being you. Keep leading well.

I have a leadership mantra that is not for everyone, but it is simply this: "Screw 'em." At some point, you have to just keep doing, being, and becoming everything you were designed to be. If people didn't create your destiny, then they can't destroy it. That's why you have to suck it up and keep going and growing! You don't need anyone's approval to walk in God's authority. Keep doing you, and suck it up no matter what. There is no difficulty that you will face that can take you out—unless you let it.

> *If people didn't create your destiny, then they can't destroy it. That's why you have to suck it up and keep going and growing!*

Now, get out there, and show the world who you are and what you can do! Be the leader God called you to be! Stand up and stand strong. The greatest of leaders will suck it up and continue to walk in their calling and destiny.

Leadership is not easy! Yes, everyone likes the titles, but they have a difficult time with the tests. Everyone loves the idea of leadership until they stand in the shoes of leadership. That's why you have to suck it up. You cannot lead long if you won't stand strong. Circle that. Highlight that. Better yet, post it on social media. You cannot lead long if you won't stand strong.

It's time to just suck it up!

UNLEASH YOUR THOUGHTS

Do you have a glass jaw, or can you take it on the chin?

_____

_____

_____

_____

_____

_____

_____

_____

_____

Do you remember a time when you had to suck it up? Explain.

_____

_____

_____

_____

_____

_____

_____

_____

_____

_____

Do you know anyone who ran away or quit their leadership because they couldn't suck it up?

_____

_____

_____

_____

_____

_____

_____

_____

_____

_____

If you struggle with receiving criticism or insults, what can you do to have a stronger jaw?

_____

_____

_____

_____

_____

_____

_____

_____

_____

_____

ELEVATION REQUIRES SEPARATION

I learned a hard lesson early in leadership: only those who grow with you will be able to go with you! Yes, that's even hard to write. If you are going to unleash your leadership, you will need to discover quickly that elevation requires separation. Not everyone will be able to go where you want to lead your business, organization, or church.

The faster you realize that some people are not designed to be long-term members of your vision, the better you will become as a leader. I heard about this concept, called "The Scaffolding Principle" about twenty years ago. The basic premise is that some people are scaffolding; they gather around you to help you put the building up, but they are not going to help you fill the building. Here's why this matters: scaffolding does not stay up forever, and people won't be around forever.

My wife and I were speaking with Phil and Jeannie Munsey several years ago. We were going through a difficult time with several key families from our church leaving. It was very painful. We will never forget what Jeannie told us: "When it comes to people, serve with open hands." That was a word that we both needed. Ever since that moment, it has been easier to serve because people come and go.

"I love when people leave my organization." Very few people say that. Or at least, I never say that! Sometimes, though, you have people in spaces and places that are actually holding your business, church, or even you back.

Yes, I am a pastor, but I am also really spiritual. That seems like a given, but to be honest, that's not always true. I believe

God speaks to me. The primary way is through His Word, the Bible, but I also believe He speaks to me on the inside. It's the Holy Spirit—God's presence in our lives. At the beginning of 2022, I felt the Holy Spirit say, *Some of your allies will become your enemies.* This was hard to grasp, but then slowly, it started to happen. People who I thought were in my corner started to attack, accuse, and insult. Someone from another church told one of our staff members, "Everybody at our church thinks your church is a cult." What? *We were— are—friends with that church,* I thought.

The Bible declares, "For wherever there is jealousy and selfish ambition, there you will find disorder and evil of every kind" (James 3:16). Notice that jealousy comes before the disorder. Jealousy is the enemy's way of dividing people. I have to be honest; I fight this. I often catch myself, but sometimes, I don't. I have learned that the greater the assignment, the greater the attacks! And those attacks often create separation.

Don't freak out when God starts to elevate you, but get ready because, at the same time, He will start to separate you. The higher you go, the lighter you must become. That often means letting go of some of the weight or people that have held you back.

The higher you go, the lighter you must become. That often means letting go of some of the weight or people that have held you back.

ELEVATION REQUIRES SEPARATION

As God unleashes your leadership, not everyone will accept, celebrate, or acknowledge it. That's okay. Keep growing. Don't look back. Leadership is all about elevation. As your leadership begins to go higher, not every person is going to cheer you on. When the people in your world start to see your leadership rise, get ready. Separation is next.

The leaders who are okay with the hard pill of separation are the ones who will experience elevation. If you are unwilling to walk away from people and places, you may never achieve your purpose.

As I have experienced the small measure of influence God has allowed into my life, I have noticed how people have done two things: back up and backbite. They will back up from supporting and celebrating you, but then I noticed how that moves quickly into backbiting. They will go behind your back and put knives in from every direction.

When people walk away or walk out on you, just know that you are in great company. People even walked away from Jesus. If people abandoned Jesus, they will abandon you too. Smile. As your leadership gets unleashed, you will experience some levels of separation, so you can walk in next-level elevation.

UNLEASH YOUR THOUGHTS

Can you identify those who have grown with you? Who are they?

_____

_____

_____

_____

_____

_____

_____

_____

_____

How about those you have served with open hands and are no longer with you?

_____

_____

_____

_____

_____

_____

_____

_____

_____

From what or whom do you need to separate in your life and ministry in order to be elevated?

_____

_____

_____

_____

_____

_____

_____

_____

_____

_____

_____

YOUR WHO DETERMINES YOUR YOU

My mother used to always tell me, "Don't let your friends choose you. You choose your friends." I have tried to live that principle for my entire life. What my mom was saying is that just because people want to be your friend doesn't mean they have to be because your "who" determines your "you." This will be a constant battle in your life and leadership!

> *Just because people want to be part of your circle doesn't mean you have to let them be because your "who" determines your "you."*

Your circle determines your cycle. Whom you surround yourself with matters. If you are always hanging out with negative people, you will become negative. If you find yourself spending time with critical people, then you will start to lean toward the critical side too. It's just the natural progression of relationships.

My wife and I have things that we do or think that are different, but the longer we are together, the more we think similarly to each other. Notice that I said similarly—not identically. We still have things we see a bit differently, but the more time we spend with each other, the more we start to reflect each other. The same is true of your circle. You will always become like those you spend the most time with.

Your who matters. So, even though this is not the best grammar, make sure that you have the right who next to you!

This is true of your personal and professional lives. With that being said, you have to be the right you too. (Say that five times fast.) Why? Because you can't be the who everyone else is avoiding! Raise your leadership by being the who you want to surround yourself with.

The question has to be, *What kind of person do I want to be?* Great question. I am so glad you are thinking that right now! Here are a few characteristics that become attractive for people to follow:

- Be positive. People are drawn to those who believe, "We can do it!" more than those who believe, "It's impossible."
- Be encouraging. Choose to lift the spirits of those around you. It is vital to unleashing your leadership.
- Be excellent. That's more than a Bill and Ted reference. It really should drive our lives to do things with excellence.
- Be consistent. Don't live life on the ups and downs. Be consistent in every area and arena.
- Be vocal. Share your opinion. People respect that. Just make sure they respect you after you share it.
- Be generous. Be willing to share your time, your knowledge, your resources, and your life with those around you.

There are many more attractive qualities, but that's a start. Simply be the who that you want to attract because your who determines your you.

I have never really gone after people or pushed open doors just to "know" certain people. God has brought these specific people into my life. Don't go in pursuit of people, influencers, and/or investors for the purpose of using or profiting from them. They will spot that from a mile away. Just be the best version of you, and the right people will come into your life at the right time.

Surround yourself with the right people, put yourself in the right places, and the right things will take place.

UNLEASH YOUR THOUGHTS

Name five people who are part of your circle.

_____

_____

_____

_____

_____

What are your criteria for allowing people to be a part of your circle?

_____

_____

_____

_____

_____

_____

_____

_____

_____

_____

_____

_____

_____

_____

How can you become the best version of you? What might you need to embrace or reject?

_____

_____

_____

_____

_____

_____

_____

_____

_____

_____

_____

_____

_____

_____

_____

_____

DON'T MISTAKE AN INVITE FOR YOUR CALLING

Not every invitation we get should be accepted. From the very outset of our leadership, we have to discover our calling. Our calling is the unique thing that God has placed us on planet Earth to do. Every single person on the planet has a calling, whether they admit it or not. Once you determine your calling, it is easier to say yes or no to other people's requests.

As a leader, people will ask you all the time for favors. It's just human nature—especially as your success begins to grow. Hear me loud and clear. Are you listening? You don't have to say yes to everything. If you do, then you might miss the right thing you should be doing.

Remember in chapter 2, when we talked about every moment mattering, so I declined the invitation to attend that conference? Well, you are not called to everything you get invited to! If you are, then your motivation is probably not your calling. Be cautious in what you say yes to because that one yes could keep you from the thing you should actually be doing or attending. Don't take the bait. Follow your calling.

> *Be cautious in what you say yes to because that one yes could keep you from the thing you should actually be doing or attending.*

I am going to share some brutal, honest truth with you. I hope you are ready. Most people accept every invitation because they are looking for validation. Okay, take a moment to process that. Being able to say, "I was invited to speak here," or "I was invited to dinner with so and so," can be exciting, but not every opportunity is part of your design.

Some of these accepted invites are more a matter of pride than purpose. I know for me, I have had to struggle with that from time to time. Nah, more often than that. When a peer invites us to something large-scale, it can easily stroke our ego.

At the end of 2019, I received an invitation to speak at C3 Conference in Dallas, Texas, with Pastor Ed Young Jr. The invitation was for 2021, but they wanted to create a promotion to advertise at their 2020 conference. Well, my ego got brushed a little bit. It felt surreal, and if I am honest, my pride swelled a little. God has a way of humbling us: COVID-19 hit! Other circumstances arose, and I was not invited back (or at least not yet). After I found out I was not speaking, my son said to me, "Dad, it doesn't matter. That does not help us build our church." That gentle reminder pushed me back to my calling. So, now I humbly celebrate that I am a C3-invited speaker. (Hey, if someone can say they were nominated for a Grammy, why can't I claim this one?)

Not every invitation is part of your calling. Most invites are not wrong, but make sure that God has really called you to whatever environment you find yourself in. If it ain't God, your pride will swell up.

UNLEASH YOUR THOUGHTS

How can you identify your calling?

_____
_____
_____
_____
_____
_____
_____
_____
_____

Can you state your calling? What is it?

_____
_____
_____
_____
_____
_____
_____
_____
_____
_____

When have you made decisions or accepted invitations based on your calling?

_____

_____

_____

_____

_____

_____

_____

_____

_____

_____

_____

_____

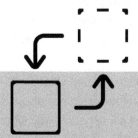

DON'T TAKE ADVICE FROM SOMEONE YOU WOULDN'T TRADE PLACES WITH

"**D**on't take advice from someone you wouldn't trade places with." This principle sounds harsh at first, but the simplicity of its truth is actually profound. Don't take advice from someone you would not trade places with. Would you take marriage advice from someone on their fifth marriage? Would you receive business advice from someone who has filed for bankruptcy in every business they started? The answer is no. Or at least, it should be a hard "NO."

This does not mean you can't learn from everybody. In fact, I can learn from anybody. It's not about size, popularity, or talent! There are just some people with whom you would never want to trade places because their life, leadership, business, or organization is a wreck. Sadly, those are the ones who are always offering advice to everybody!

There are a few types of people everyone can learn from, though. First, learn from those who are learners! Surround yourself with people who are always growing and pushing the limits on their growth. Don't settle for the settlers. Get some people in your circle that are continually learning.

Second, learn from those who are successful. Now, success is subjective. That's why this matters. If you believe someone is successful, then you get to determine if they are a person you can learn from.

> *Whom you take advice from will determine what kind of advice you get. So, you have to be extremely careful about whom you allow to speak into your life.*

Whom you take advice from will determine what kind of advice you get. So, you have to be extremely careful about whom you allow to speak into your life.

There are a ton of people who love to give advice. Guard against those people. Too many people want to give you advice about your money, your marriage, your kids, your job, and/or your calling, but they are not doing any of those things well. Be cautious with advice experts.

Third, learn from those who are humble. Yes, make sure that you are not listening to the high and mighty. Dial in to the simple and humble. One of my favorite leaders on the planet is a pastor named Mark Batterson. He is extremely successful: he's a *New York Times* best-selling author, pastors a mega-church, and is invited to speak all over the world. Yet Mark is one of the most humble people I have ever met. I can learn from that guy any day of the week!

The Bible reveals that pride is the ultimate killer of our potential. That's why we need to surround ourselves with the humble. This will cause us to remain humble.

Finally, learn from those who are full of integrity. This is vital. It's not just what you learn; it's whom you are learning from.

Attitude influences attitude. Spirit infects spirit. Character shapes character.

I have met a lot of people who were one thing publicly and a different thing privately. I try and be the same person—always. I am not a genetically modified leader. I am what I am, and that's what I am. I'll give you the advice I would actually take! Pause. Ask yourself, *Who is giving me this advice?* This question is vital if you want to unleash your leadership because many leaders get stuck where they are because they only take advice from people who are merely advice givers.

Let me finish this lesson with some practical thoughts about leadership circles. Many leaders surround themselves with environments that choke their potential. They serve under leaders or alongside leaders where they are constantly thinking, *Why am I still here?* If you are asking yourself that question, it's time for a change.

I have personally had to walk away from networks or reduce time in those networks to surround myself with leaders I want to learn from or emulate. Some circles will actually limit your growth potential because they are not growing. Stifling leaders will always stifle other leaders. Hey, if you are not willing to trade places with them, why would you take advice from them?

This lesson does not mean you can't learn from anyone. However, you must make it a priority to have your circle made up of people you dream of being like. If you need more passion, get around some passionate people. If you need to be better at making decisions, surround yourself with strong decision-makers. And remember this, advice from the unsuccessful usually leads to unsuccessful places. Refuse to take advice from someone you would not trade places with!

UNLEASH YOUR THOUGHTS

Identify people in your life that you've taken advice from.

_____

_____

_____

_____

_____

_____

_____

_____

_____

Would you trade places with each one of those people?

_____

_____

_____

_____

_____

_____

_____

_____

_____

_____

Who are the five people in your life who meet the adviser criteria: learners, successful, humble, and have integrity?

_____

_____

_____

_____

_____

_____

_____

_____

_____

_____

_____

_____

_____

_____

_____

IMPOSSIBLE IS ONLY IMPOSSIBLE UNTIL SOMEONE DOES THE IMPOSSIBLE

Impossible. People love taking on the impossible. I remember when Mary and I were about to start our church on Long Island, New York. There hadn't been a successful church plant in our denomination in nearly twenty years. I had pastor-friends tell me, "That's impossible. You are going to ruin your reputation if it doesn't work." Very few people were cheering us on at the beginning. We had people behind us, but the majority were nervous about our journey.

Impossible is overcome by taking risks!

Well, to all the doubters in 2008, we are still going, baby! Impossible is only impossible until someone does the impossible! My family and I have built a great church that is growing, going, and sowing!

The Bible declares that "with God all things are possible" (Matthew 19:26). In other words, it may be impossible with you, but nothing is impossible when God gets involved! Let me write that again: *nothing is impossible when God gets involved.*

Don't live life with excuses or regrets! Start that business. Launch that nonprofit. Ask that girl to marry you. Yes, she may be out of your league, but nothing is impossible with God. After all, it's only impossible until someone does the impossible.

Impossible is overcome by taking risks, but during the pandemic that started in 2020, we lost our risk-taking drive. We have become more passive than aggressive. It's time to start taking some risks again. Don't let life beat the drive to try out of your spirit. Take your life back. Start dreaming again.

I was a cheer-lifter at Central Bible College for part of a basketball season when I was younger. There are not many cheers I remember. To be honest, I only remember two. But here's one: "Be aggressive. Be. Be aggressive. Be aggressive. Be. Be aggressive." Get aggressive about living the life God has called you to.

A pandemic or a problem cannot stop your purpose. You were placed on planet Earth for a bigger reason than walking around aimlessly waiting to safely arrive at death. No, God has a bigger purpose for you. Don't let the word *impossible* scare you!

It was impossible to fly until the Wright brothers did it. It is scientifically impossible for a bee to fly—its wings are too small, and its body too fat. But nobody told the bee it was impossible. Friend, catch this today: it's only impossible until someone does the impossible!

Don't let fear paralyze you. Stop making excuses, and start making a difference. Today is a great day to do the impossible.

Forget the haters. Ignore the doubters.

Do the impossible!

UNLEASH YOUR THOUGHTS

What has been one impossible thing you've seen God do through you?

_____

_____

_____

_____

_____

_____

_____

_____

_____

_____

What is one goal or dream that seems impossible to you right now?

_____

_____

_____

_____

_____

_____

_____

_____

_____

_____

_____

How can you be aggressive in pursuing this dream or goal?

_____

_____

_____

_____

_____

_____

_____

_____

_____

_____

_____

_____

_____

_____

_____

_____

_____

_____

_____

_____

_____

_____

WHAT GOT YOU HERE WILL NOT GET YOU THERE

As our church started growing, my wife and I were not able to do everything that we did when we first started it. At fifty people, it was easy to call people, but at five hundred, it became nearly impossible to lead the same way. One of our closest friends decided to leave the church. They did not say anything to us. They just picked up and left. They may have ignored us, but they told others, "They are not the same people as when we first came to church."

My response was, "That's good. If I am the same leader five years later, then I am not the right leader."

You see, what brought you to where you are is not the same thing that will take you to where you need to be.

I am not talking about character change. I am talking about style, not substance. Our character should always be full of integrity. I am not talking about cutting corners, but true, personal growth.

You see, as your business or organization grows, you will have to grow too. Your style of leadership may have to change. "Noooooooooooo!" You may be screaming right now. In a small business, it is easier to be a hands-on leader, but if your company grows into a Fortune 500 one, you have to be a stronger delegator. Every level your leadership goes up will require you to elevate your leadership. If you do not, you will become the lid to your organization, nonprofit, or church.

> *If you are not the same leader as you were*
> *five years ago, throw yourself a party.*

If you are not the same leader as you were five years ago, throw yourself a party.

Change is required for any business or leader to continue to innovate. Your personality may be able to grow a business to a million in revenue. However, an ability to raise up other leaders will be necessary to build that ten-million-dollar-per-year company. Style, attitude, approach, staff, and more will be needed if you want to grow to the next level.

I have had to change how I lead over the last four years. As our church started to hit a leadership lid, I began to blame everything and everybody else. But that did not change a thing. Then I started to look within. Mary and I co-lead our church, and I realized that her leadership style is better than mine when it comes to sustaining continual growth. Her philosophy is simple, "I tell people what I would like, and they have the responsibility to accomplish it." Then she gives them the freedom and finances to do it. Me? I was a control freak.

Since then, I have become much more trusting and permission-giving, and we have watched our church grow in ways we could never imagine. I had to change. If I had stayed the same as a leader, there would be no one to blame but me. We still would be at the same place we were four years ago.

Here's the reality: just when you think you have mastered your level, you will need to adjust again to reach the next level. In fact, leadership is the constant ability to adapt and grow as your organization does. Don't be the lid to your leadership.

Change is a priority for continued growth. No one can just cruise into every new level. At some point, every leader has to make a decision to keep pushing the limits. After all, growth is not accidental; it is intentional!

Where do you need to make adjustments? Every leader either adjusts or becomes irrelevant. One of the most iconic female singers of all time is Madonna. Her music spanned over three decades. Why? She made adjustments to the style and substance of her music. You may or may not agree with me, but I promise you that she has been iconic.

Here are the Ps that need to constantly change in order to get to the next level:

- People—There may be moments when you need some new people in your life to rise higher.
- Places—Leaders know that not every place is the right place for them.
- Paper—A leader's attitude toward money and actions with money will constantly need to grow.
- Priorities—For every level of leadership, you will need to evaluate your priorities and goals.

Unleash your leadership, and grow to the next level because what got you here will not get you there!

UNLEASH YOUR THOUGHTS

How are you a different leader now than you were five years ago?

_____

_____

_____

_____

_____

_____

_____

_____

_____

_____

When have you been a lid to someone else?

_____

_____

_____

_____

_____

_____

_____

_____

_____

_____

What are some things you need to change now to propel you into the next five years of leadership?

_____

_____

_____

_____

_____

_____

_____

_____

_____

_____

_____

_____

_____

_____

_____

_____

_____

A FIRE NEEDS THREE THINGS TO BURN

A FIRE NEEDS THREE THINGS TO BURN

When I was growing up, our family took a lot of camping trips. I was not a fan, but my mom wanted to do it, so we did. Incidentally, during the last camping trip that our family went on, a skunk got into our tent, and we all got sprayed. End of camping. I was forever grateful for that skunk.

Over the years, though, we had to build a lot of fires while on those trips. A fire needs three simple things to burn: oxygen, heat, and fuel. These are essential elements. Take one out, and the fire goes out. Your leadership is the same. It really requires three things: potential (oxygen), passion (heat), and purpose (fuel).

Potential—This is the capacity to actually do what you are planning to do. Some people overestimate their potential. Discover your skills and talents, add hard work, and you will have a good shot at adding oxygen to a fire.

Passion—Do you have that burning desire to lay it all on the line for your calling, business, church, or organization? Can your passion ignite someone else's passion? You see, passion is catchy. You must have passion as a leader if you want to create a fire through your leadership.

Purpose—This is all about the endgame. Purpose is the goal you have set out to accomplish. Your purpose always determines the people you will attract. If your purpose does not make a difference in people's lives, you will attract the lethargic and lazy.

A fire is a critical component of your leadership's success. What? A fire? Yes. A thousand times, yes! People come to watch something burn. Sometimes, I start a fire in my firepit in the backyard, and I just stare into the mesmerizing flames. A fire grabs attention. Your potential, your passion, and your purpose will get people's attention.

Don't hide the fire that God has placed in you. Let it become visible. Don't apologize for it. Every employee or coworker needs to see the fire burning deep in your heart. Why? Because fire spreads!

> *Every employee or coworker needs to see the fire burning deep in your heart. Why? Because fire spreads!*

Every business needs, from time to time, a fresh fire lit under every employee. And, yes, even churches need fresh fire to keep their purpose alive.

Many leaders run from fire, but let yourself be drawn to it—to see why it's burning, growing, expanding, and building. Don't criticize someone else's fire, but let that fire ignite something in your life and leadership.

Get your fire back! Unleash your potential! Ignite your passion.

Find your purpose.

You are just getting started. Strike the match today. Don't wait. Light that fire in your leadership.

UNLEASH YOUR THOUGHTS

How do you know if potential, passion, and purpose are operating to keep your fire burning?

_____

_____

_____

_____

_____

_____

_____

_____

_____

Which one is lacking? Why?

_____

_____

_____

_____

_____

_____

_____

_____

_____

_____

Is your potential clear?

_____

_____

_____

_____

What is your passion?

_____

_____

_____

_____

_____

_____

What is your purpose?

_____

_____

_____

_____

_____

_____

_____

DON'T PLAY THE VICTIM CARD

L et me hit this right away—there are victims. Yes, there are people who have been deceived, abused, neglected, mistreated, and more. This is not about that. Those issues need to be addressed, and those people need healing. That's not the victim I am discussing.

Some leaders always play the victim. "Everyone is out to get me," or "Everybody is against me," are the mantras of a leader playing the victim card. The reality is you cannot say, "Everybody is against me," because everybody does not know you! A leader who uses the victim card is really using the manipulation card. They want people to feel sorry for them, so those people rally around them. That's just poor leadership.

> *Leaders who play the victim card want people to feel sorry for them, so those people rally around them. That's just poor leadership.*

People rarely rally around people who play the victim card, but they do rally around a vision calling. It may seem hard to believe, but the attention people receive as they cry, "I am a victim," only lasts so long. Vision, though, lasts beyond circumstances. Leaders who are constantly playing the victim card will leave a trail of victims. It is just a natural consequence.

How do you know if you are playing the victim card? Great question. The number one way, in my opinion, is to analyze your words and behavior. You will always head in the direction of what you put on repeat. So, if your language is always, "People don't like me," or "Everyone is against me," then you are going to fall into the snare of playing the victim.

I grew up in poverty. I saw abuse in our home. I personally experienced verbal abuse. I was bullied in elementary school. I could play the victim in a heartbeat. Screw that.

Yes, you read that! Screw the victim card. It ain't worth playing. God did not make me a victim. Scripture declares, "No, despite all these things, overwhelming victory is ours through Christ, who loved us" (Romans 8:37). This verse and many others demonstrate you are not a victim but a victor—despite all of "these things." The apostle Paul, who wrote that passage, presents a huge list of hardships. In other words, no matter what you face, despite it all, overwhelming victory is yours. It belongs to you!

As a leader, it is vital to lead with a victor mentality. People are attracted to it, but they are also inspired by it. Victim mentality attracts, too, but it attracts other victims. When you lead with a victor attitude, you will attract other victors. Leaders who want to excel and grow will naturally want to be around you!

Our culture elevates those who have the biggest victim card, but leaders elevate those who lead with a victory mindset. Push the limits. Keep grinding. Don't let labels limit you. Lift your leadership out of the valley of victimhood and onto the mountain of victory.

If I were to look into my past, I could find a million excuses to fail. However, I choose not to focus on what happened to me but on what God has done through me. Real leadership is not a slogan, mantra, or statement. It is the ability to rise above the negativity and step into your destiny.

Now, get up, and start climbing. Victory is before you!

UNLEASH YOUR THOUGHTS

Be honest. Have you been playing the victim card?

_____

_____

_____

_____

_____

_____

_____

_____

_____

_____

What made you a victim?

_____

_____

_____

_____

_____

_____

_____

_____

_____

_____

_____

What have you overcome?

_____

_____

_____

_____

_____

_____

_____

_____

_____

_____

What are some ways you can change your language from victim to victor?

_____

_____

_____

_____

_____

_____

_____

_____

_____

_____

LEADERSHIP IS SLOW-COOKED, NEVER MICROWAVED

I love pot roast. That's a fact. What the heck does that have to do with leadership? Everything.

The microwave was developed—by accident—in 1945 by Percy Spencer. Yes, you read that right! It was an accident. While working with a defense company on a radar system, Spencer noticed his chocolate bar melted during a test. Up until that point, things had taken time to cook.

Leadership takes time to cook too. No one leaps from obscurity into popularity. It takes days, weeks, months, and years of development that no one sees.

> *Leadership takes time to cook too. It takes days, weeks, months, and years of development that no one sees.*

Back to pot roast. You can't prepare a good pot roast in a microwave. It takes time. In fact, it could take anywhere from three to six hours to do it right! A lot of leaders want to be noticed and recognized after days of leading, but it takes years of leadership for God to elevate your life.

Leadership is not accidental; it is intentional. That means every minute and every moment is preparation. The good, the bad, and the ugly seasons of life are getting you ready for your destiny. And that destiny is often cooked slowly.

Are you getting hungry yet? Is your mouth starting to water for some slow-cooked leadership?

I have watched a lot of leaders over the years attempt to microwave their leadership by pushing their way to the top and trying to force doors to open. Forcing a door open is microwave leadership. Allowing God to open the door is slow-cooked leadership.

Microsoft was started in 1974 in a garage. Dell began in a garage in 1985. The idea for Google started in a garage. Amazon began in Jeff Bezos's garage. What's the point? Find a garage, and start something. The success of these businesses did not start on Wall Street but on Main Street. None of these companies had any idea what they were creating when they started, but look at how they revolutionized their industries. Leadership takes time!

Here's some advice:

- Don't rush the process.
- Take your time developing yourself. The faster you rise—the quicker you can fall.
- Let God build your resume, and then watch how fast time feels like it is moving!

Some leaders operate by pressure. They set unrealistic goals and timelines. Others lead according to their purpose. I believe it takes both of those, but sometimes we put too much pressure to perform on our leadership. Set your purpose, and let God chart your course! It may seem like it is taking longer than you want, but God is using this time to prepare you.

LEADERSHIP IS SLOW-COOKED, NEVER MICROWAVED

Just like a good pot roast, the longer God takes to prepare you, the deeper your leadership flavor will be. Don't stress about the process. Just walk in your purpose.

Now, start celebrating your slow-cooked leadership!

UNLEASH YOUR THOUGHTS

What are you microwaving in your leadership that needs to be cooked slowly?

_____

_____

_____

_____

_____

_____

_____

_____

_____

What doors have you forced open?

_____

_____

_____

_____

_____

_____

_____

_____

_____

Are you intentionally preparing for the door God wants to open in your leadership? How?

_____

_____

_____

_____

_____

_____

_____

_____

_____

_____

_____

_____

_____

_____

_____

_____

LESSON EIGHTEEN

SCREW WHAT OTHER PEOPLE THINK

I am a New Yorker. So, pardon the language, but this principle is true. If you are called to lead, you are going to have to screw what other people think. The moment you step out in front of the pack is when criticism and cynicism are launched at you. The biggest critics are usually the least influential. Most of the social media hate I have endured has come from people with five followers (maybe a few more, but you get the point). As a pastor, I have had people threaten to leave the church and take people with them. When they left, they left. Massive crowds did not follow the critics. Screw what people think.

> *I learned this concept years ago: if I make God happy, then it does not matter who else I make unhappy.*

Scripture declares, "Obviously, I'm not trying to win the approval of people, but of God. If pleasing people were my goal, I would not be Christ's servant" (Galatians 1:10). I learned this concept years ago: if I make God happy, then it does not matter who else I make unhappy. I may stand before people on social media, but I will stand before God in eternity. Screw what other people think.

This does not give me permission to hurt people. That's not leadership. However, at some point, I have had to do what God has called me to do regardless of people's opinions! This also does not give me permission to violate true accountability.

This is going to sound bananas. Not everyone's opinion should matter to you, but there are many that you should be concerned about. Therefore, this leadership principle is not a license to be an egotistical jerk.

In several relationships, you, as a leader, must be open to healthy critique: your spouse (if you're married), your team, your accountability relationships, and your most trusted friends. However, not everyone on the planet should be given permission to speak into your life! That is not healthy. Surround yourself with the right accountability, and you will run toward your destiny.

I am far from a people pleaser. You may be the same way. In fact, if you are a true leader, pleasing people is the furthest thing from your mind. Still, when people say stuff about us on social media or send us a nasty email, it is often hurtful. Moving beyond what other people think is not about hating on them or mistreating them. It is about loving your destiny and treating your dreams like they matter. Hey, if God gave them to you, they must be pretty valuable!

What is true accountability? It is the permission you give to people you trust and respect to speak correction into your life. This is vital. Most leaders' limits will be due to a lack of real accountability! Find the right people. Give them permission to speak candidly and honestly. Beyond that, screw what other people think.

When you live the dream God has called you to live, there will be haters, doubters, and skeptics. That's okay. Don't attack them. Just move on. They did not create your destiny, and their negativity cannot stop it.

Now, stop reading and ask yourself: *Am I living to please people, or am I living to please God?*

UNLEASH YOUR THOUGHTS

Has your leadership been criticized? In what way?

_____
_____
_____
_____
_____
_____
_____
_____
_____

How did it affect how you lead?

_____
_____
_____
_____
_____
_____
_____
_____
_____
_____

SCREW WHAT OTHER PEOPLE THINK

Which people are in your RIGHT accountability relationships?

_____

_____

_____

_____

_____

_____

_____

_____

_____

_____

_____

Without hurting anyone, what is one way you said, "Screw 'em," moved on, and did what truly mattered?

_____

_____

_____

_____

_____

_____

_____

_____

_____

_____

COMFORT IS THE ENEMY OF PROGRESS

My bride, Mary, always says, "God did not call us to a comfortable life but to live an uncomfortably comfortable life." I echo that 100 percent. Most of the greatest advancements that have been achieved are because someone stepped out of their comfort zone. Air travel, or even space travel, happens because someone took a risk.

Electricity.

Steam power.

Laser surgery.

> *Most advancements come on the backside of discomfort. In leadership, it is vital that you never get stuck in comfort.*

Most advancements come on the backside of discomfort. In leadership, it is vital that you never get stuck in comfort. As leadership guru Kenny Loggins once sang, "I'll take you right into the danger zone."[2] Real leaders may not like the danger zone, but they also don't avoid it.

If we are comfortable on the sidelines, we'll remain on the sidelines. If we are comfortable being average, we'll settle for average every time. That's why we have to break out of the cage of comfort. Every leader faces tension at multiple points in their leadership: How much comfort is too much? How

---

2 Kenny Loggins, vocalist, "Danger Zone," by Giorgio Moroder and Tom Whitlock, released May 13, 1986, track 1 on *Top Gun*, Columbia Records.

much risk is too great? A friend of mine—Mark Batterson—says, "Playing it safe is risky." I happen to agree.

Don't allow the comfort of success to keep you from your next successful venture, opportunity, or risk.

Ted Young started his painting company by painting his neighbor's shed just so he could buy groceries. Before he knew it, he was painting one house and another. Twenty years later, that risk has paid off with a successful business. He wrote, "Taking a risk impacted my life in that something came from nothing, and we are still benefiting from that risk-taking behavior to this day."[3]

Comfort is the avoidance of risk. I have learned that if we want our leadership unleashed, we can't avoid risk, and we can't choose comfort. Everything we do in life has a risk factor to it. So, why do we play it safe? Why do we find ourselves doing the mundane instead of the monumental? I believe it's because most leaders would rather appear to be a success than to appear a failure.

Akio Morita co-founded Sony. Their first product was a rice cooker. The only problem was that it burned the rice. That did not stop Sony from becoming a worldwide innovator. Colonel Sanders was rejected a thousand times before one restaurant accepted his secret chicken recipe. Oh yeah, he launched Kentucky Fried Chicken when he was sixty-five

---

3 Julie Scheidegger, "Eight Readers Share Their Stories of Taking Risks," *Ewing Marion Kauffman Foundation*, 16 Jan. 2020, https://www.kauffman.org/currents/eight-readers-share-their-stories-of-taking-risks/.

years old. What's the point? It's never too late to step out of your comfort zone.

Every leader knows that comfort is the enemy of progress, so it is imperative to raise your risk threshold (your willingness to fail) so that you can achieve your God-given dreams. When you start to get comfortable, do something to shake yourself out of your comfort zone. Take a risk. Try something new.

If you are willing to risk a failure, you may find yourself celebrating a magnificent success!

UNLEASH YOUR THOUGHTS

Is your leadership becoming comfortable? How might you be playing it safe?

_____

_____

_____

_____

_____

_____

_____

_____

_____

_____

How are you stepping out of your comfort zone?

_____

_____

_____

_____

_____

_____

_____

_____

_____

_____

What are some risks you are willing to take TODAY?

_____
_____
_____
_____
_____
_____
_____
_____
_____
_____
_____
_____
_____
_____

IF YOU CAN'T HANDLE THE ATTACKS YOU WON'T HANDLE THE ASSIGNMENT

Every leader who has ever been unleashed has faced attacks. Oh yes, I learned very young that it is not the back of the pack that faces the attack; it's the front of the line every time. It's when we start to become everything God designed us to be that there will be skirmishes from multiple sides. Therefore, "If you can't handle the attacks, you won't handle the assignment" is a vital concept for anyone who aspires to be a leader to grab onto. A leader who thinks leadership is a tiptoe through the tulips is going to have an eye-opening first day on the job.

> *"If you can't handle the attacks, you won't handle the assignment" is a vital concept for anyone who aspires to be a leader to grab onto.*

Leaders face mountains of criticism. All the time. It's a fact of leadership. If we cannot handle the onslaught of the onlookers, we may never walk into our greatest days. We just have to embrace the attacks, criticisms, and complaints that come with leadership.

So, how does a person handle the attacks when they come? That's the million-dollar question. And it's never *if* they come; it's *when* they come. First, I believe you have to accept the reality that criticism just comes with the job. It doesn't matter if you are leading your children or a Fortune 500 company. Critics will always come out of the woodwork.

In order to handle the attacks, you just have to know they are going to happen. No matter how good you are, they are still part of leadership.

Second, you have to learn to respond—not react—to the attacks. This is huge. Most leaders react. They get defensive, angry, agitated, frustrated, and knee-jerky. It's like we said in Chapter 8: "Suck It Up," a true leader cannot lead with a glass jaw.

Responding to criticism or attacks, whether they are fair or not, starts with a listening ear. At some point, you need to shift from being angry to answering questions. You will need to move from looking away from a problem to leaning in to find a solution.

Third, know that you get what you allow. If the attacks are unfounded and you allow them to happen, you cannot complain when they get compounded. In other words, more and more people begin the onslaught. It is your job, as a leader, to bring immediate correction when someone is gossiping, hyper-critical, or negative about your leadership or organization.

Finally, recognize that when you are called, nothing can take you off your assignment. This is what motivates me each day. I am called to do exactly what I am doing today. Whether you are a stay-at-home parent, a CEO, a manager, or a store clerk, you are where God designed you to be right now. That does not mean you will always be there, but God has put you there right now. Somewhere in this book or in your journal, write down in all caps, I AM CALLED. Keep walking in that calling. Stand on it. Trust it.

God did not bring you this far in life to allow your leadership to slow down. In fact, God is just getting started. The more your leadership gets unleashed, the more the attacks will come. And the greater your capacity for pain, the greater the tenacity of your purpose.

Let me say this: don't go pursuing attacks. Some leaders cultivate a culture of division. It's almost as if the attacks are self-designed. Don't be that leader. Be the leader who recognizes the attacks but does not enjoy them.

UNLEASH YOUR THOUGHTS

Has your leadership been attacked? How?

_____

_____

_____

_____

_____

_____

_____

_____

_____

_____

How did you handle the attack? What would you have done differently?

_____

_____

_____

_____

_____

_____

_____

_____

_____

_____

_____

IF YOU CAN'T HANDLE THE ATTACKS YOU WON'T HANDLE THE ASSIGNMENT

Have you brought correction when the attacks are unfounded and hyper-critical? How?

_____

_____

_____

_____

_____

_____

_____

_____

_____

_____

_____

_____

_____

_____

_____

_____

_____

EVEN DEAD FISH CAN SWIM DOWNSTREAM

I used to go fishing when I lived in upstate New York. It was freshwater fishing in a lot of streams and lakes. I learned something while fishing in the Hudson River. If you are old enough, you might remember that several companies released chemicals way north into the Hudson River that polluted the environment and wildlife. As a matter of fact, we used to have a saying: "Never eat the three-eyed fish you catch in the Hudson—throw it back." Periodically, I would fish on the current, and there were a lot of times that a dead fish would just go floating by. What does all this have to do with leadership? Everything. Because while your business or organization is riding your momentum, there are going to be some employees that are flowing with you, but they are not growing with you!

I have a leadership expression I have said for decades. I am sure it's not original, but here it is: if you can't grow with us, you won't be able to go with us. Since a dead fish is only going to distract you from catching living fish, it stands to reason that dead leaders will keep you from developing living leaders. Don't allow the people in your church, business, or organization to feel like they can just float along. Your job is to motivate people to your mission. If people can't be motivated, they should be terminated. I'm not talking Arnold Schwarzenegger terminated—just reassigned.

As your organization starts to gain traction, it will attract a lot of dead fish who simply want a resume sticker. They want to use your brand to elevate their name, so be cautious when hiring people.

I heard this quote years ago: "The more time you spend in selection, the less time you will spend with infection." Oooooh, let's stop here for a minute and drill down. Many leaders are struggling to discover why their business or nonprofit is not taking off. They've got the right vision, and they are the right leader. The problem is that they also have a staff infection. They've allowed someone on their watch to infect the rest of the staff with laziness and lethargy. The longer you let that person stay on your team, the more people will get infected by their behavior and attitude.

> *I have a simple policy in hiring: Hire slowly. Fire quickly.*

I have a simple policy in hiring: Hire slowly. Fire quickly. Take your time in the hiring process. Hire a team to vet all future employees. Build a relationship. Check their resume. Call their references. Let me say it this way: just because someone worked for a big company doesn't mean they *worked* for a big company. And if you hire the wrong person, at some point, you just have to rip the Band-Aid off and treat the issue that it has been covering up—a staff infection. Fire quickly!

I know several business leaders who have a hard time firing people. I remember the first time I ever had to do it. Oh, how I wrestled with it! But then, I spoke to my friend Jeff, and he said, "I have never fired anyone; they fire themselves." Now, I recognize it's an individual's behavior, attitude, and ability that determine their level of competency. If they don't have what it takes, it is my responsibility to release them. Here's the good news: releasing them might be the best thing for them and for us because it pushes them in a new direction.

Never forget: even dead fish can swim downstream. Simple advice: let them swim past you!

UNLEASH YOUR THOUGHTS

Are you creating momentum through your leadership?

_____

_____

_____

_____

_____

_____

_____

_____

_____

Have you noticed individuals who are just along for the ride? How have you motivated them?

_____

_____

_____

_____

_____

_____

_____

_____

_____

_____

What does your hiring process look like? Does it build relationship?

_____

_____

_____

_____

_____

_____

_____

_____

_____

_____

_____

What was the reason you had to let a dead fish go?

_____

_____

_____

_____

_____

_____

_____

_____

_____

_____

_____

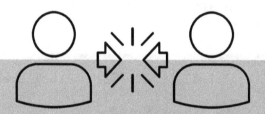

WHAT YOU DON'T CONFRONT YOU CAN'T CORRECT

don't mind confrontation. It's true. But I don't like it either! Some leaders confuse the two statements. Just because I *don't mind* doing it does not mean I *enjoy* doing it. As a lifelong New Yorker, confrontation is just part of life. Most people don't understand New Yorkers. They think we are unfriendly, but we are just direct. It saves us time. We are busy. The challenge is that most leaders are quick at direction but slow at correction.

> *If you can't self-confront, you will never self-correct. That's just a fact of leadership.*

If you can't self-confront, you will never self-correct. That's just a fact of leadership. Leaders have to look within themselves to see what they need to change in order to become better leaders in their sphere of influence. Therefore, one's hunger—or lack of hunger—to self-confront is a challenge. Every leader has the daunting tasks of examining their leadership, confronting their issues, and making the necessary changes. The leader that is able to do that will continue to unleash their leadership. The leader who does not self-correct will self-destruct!

John C. Maxwell was asked one time, "What has been your greatest challenge as a leader?" His response silenced the crowd: "Leading myself." He went on to say that it had always been that way for him. I have discovered that if we can't lead ourselves, we will probably have a difficult time leading others because what we fail to confront in ourselves, we will fail to correct in our organizations.

Confrontation and correction always start with us.

In my early days of leadership in a local church, I had a very difficult time confronting others when they had done something a little off. It was a challenge. To be honest, I still face that challenge from time to time, but more often than not, I just speak directly to the person I need to. Most of my team can receive correction from me because they know I am also constantly correcting myself. Every leader who desires to lead well and lead long has to master the art of confrontation and correction. It's non-negotiable.

Leaders or employees in any organization that cannot handle top-down confrontation should not be in that business, church, or company. Here's my simplistic advice—let them go! You never want to feel like you are walking on eggshells around staff members. Some staff members might think they are above correction because they are "this" or "that." The moment a team member pushes back on your correcting their poor behavior, it may be time to show them the door because if you are self-correcting, but your team is not, you are actually self-destructing.

We have to be okay with confrontation. A friend of mine once said (not an original to them quote), "If you want to make everyone happy, go sell ice cream." Leaders don't just sell a product, offer a service, create a sermon, or cook food. They offer an experience, and the value of that experience can be measured according to the people called to lead.

I know confrontation is hard, but the more you do it, the easier it will become. So, start by confronting yourself. Seriously, do some self-inventory. Once you finish that—Oh, wait, you will never finish that!—you can start confronting what you see in those you lead. Remember, what you fail to confront, you fail to correct.

UNLEASH YOUR THOUGHTS

What have you had to confront recently? Did you have to make correction?

_____

_____

_____

_____

_____

_____

_____

_____

_____

When was the last time you self-confronted? What self-corrections did you have to make?

_____

_____

_____

_____

_____

_____

_____

_____

_____

How are you leading your team to self-correct as well?

_____

_____

_____

_____

_____

_____

_____

_____

_____

_____

_____

_____

_____

_____

_____

_____

_____

THE GREATEST TEST OF LEADERSHIP IS LONGEVITY

Longevity is the currency of leadership. The biblical term for this is faithfulness. Sadly, in our culture today, we don't reward faithfulness as much as we should. People abandon a ship while it's sailing to jump onto someone else's ship. I love the faithful. I love longevity.

> *Longevity is the currency of leadership. The biblical term for this is faithfulness.*

The Bible teaches, "Love bears all things, believes all things, hopes all things, endures all things" (1 Corinthians 13:7). When you love what you do, you will do it for the rest of your life—and many times you will do it at the same place. Not always, but many times.

My wife and I have been blessed with our staff at Church Unleashed. We have experienced very little turnover, and when it has happened, it's usually been at an entry-level position. I have only had to release four people over the last fifteen years. That's a pretty good number. Many of my pastor-leader friends fire that many in a month. I celebrate loyalty, and I publicly honor it.

In the summer of 2022, one of our long-standing team members decided it was time for a change. Bency had been at our church since the beginning. She and her husband, Carlos, were instrumental in the growth of our church as leaders and friends. Bency came to my office one day and told me that her time at Church Unleashed was drawing to a close. She was so respectful and honoring. It was a tough conversation for her and, to be honest, for me. Bency is like a sister to me. She had served in many positions over the years. I let her know what her last day would be.

Bency finished her journey with excellence. We honored her with gifts, lunches, and a public celebration with her entire family. The church gave her a standing ovation in all three services. We have not done this with everybody, but we will do this with and for the faithful. Here's a principle that I serve by: what gets rewarded gets repeated. If leaders reward loyalty, it will be repeated. But what I have also discovered is that many leaders honor someone they've fired more than the person who has been faithful. The fired often get severance packages. The faithful get a thank you. Honor the faithful. After all, longevity is the currency of leadership.

My wife and I have made a commitment to be the lead pastors at our church for the rest of our ministry. We ain't going anywhere (unless, of course, God moves us). Our whole church knows that. Our staff knows that. We have experienced fifteen years of miracles, growth, and blessing, and I can't wait to see what the next fifteen years look like. We are committed. The challenge with most leaders is that they are always *looking* for a better option instead of *building* the better option. If you really want to unleash your leadership, last long, serve well, and love deeply.

THE GREATEST TEST OF LEADERSHIP IS LONGEVITY

Rob Lowe once said, "To achieve longevity you will have cycles. No one gets there in one straight shot."[4] That's brilliant. Longevity is about knowing that there will be twists and turns in the journey, but you know you will arrive at your appointed destiny at just the right time.

If you are a staff member, stay committed, be loyal, and remain faithful. If you are a leader, be the example of loyalty, and honor those that honor your values. The more you honor loyalty, the more of it you will have.

---

4 Rob Lowe, *Inspiring Quotes*, https://www.inspiringquotes.us/quotes/oypF_PD8X0lh1.

UNLEASH YOUR THOUGHTS

What is the longest time you've spent in a business, church, or other position of leadership? Were you honored?

_____

_____

_____

_____

_____

_____

_____

_____

_____

Have you been honoring those who have left more than the faithful who have stayed? Why?

_____

_____

_____

_____

_____

_____

_____

_____

_____

Have you been looking more than building better options?

_____

_____

_____

_____

_____

_____

_____

_____

_____

_____

_____

_____

_____

_____

IF YOU DON'T HAVE A BACKBONE YOU SHOULDN'T HAVE A MICROPHONE

IF YOU DON'T HAVE A BACKBONE YOU SHOULDN'T HAVE A MICROPHONE

I f you don't have a backbone, you shouldn't have a microphone. If you were leading in 2020, this principle will make all the sense in the world. If you were not, let me add some context. In 2020, a pandemic swept across the globe. Countless millions became infected with COVID-19. Millions of people died. Businesses closed. Churches shut down. Schools went remote. It was a tough time to lead anything from 2020 to early 2022. When word came that America was about to face this, I made the hard decision, alongside my wife, to close the doors of our church. It started as "fifteen days to slow the spread" and became over two years of restrictions.

> *If you don't have a backbone, you shouldn't have a microphone.*

Once again, I live in New York. We got hit hard, but at some point, I could not sit on the sidelines and watch our church struggle—this time, with their mental wellness. So, I grew my backbone and reopened our church before the Governor of New York gave churches permission. I got a lot of heat. "You don't love people." "You don't care." But I was convinced in my heart that our church needed to gather. In the process, we were not just "having church." We were "being the church." We gave away thousands of meals per week over a sixteen-week period. We went into impoverished communities with semi-trucks filled with food and hygiene products.

We couldn't just sit on the sidelines. I sent letters to political leaders. I made calls to local representatives. I told other pastors, "Reopen. If you don't, people will find another place to go." Two years after the beginning of the pandemic, our church was bigger than before. We could not believe it. What were our New Yorkers attracted to? Strong leadership.

People were attracted to our backbone. Now, I wish I could say I was always strong. Walking people through loss and difficulty is never easy, but leading through a global pandemic was not in the Bible college curriculum. I can't speak for every sector, but pastors who waited six months to a year to reopen have not returned to their pre-COVID attendances. I have heard every excuse, but I believe one of the greatest problems was leaders not leading. They weakened their backbone and lost their microphone.

In the middle of the pandemic, I lost both my parents. Yes, you heard that right. I was leading my church while I was going through immense pain. I preached the Sunday after my dad died, and I wasn't even going to mention it—but my wife did. I wanted to preach the gospel. The Sunday after my mom passed away, I was interviewing Casey Beathard, whose son was murdered in 2019, about facing loss. It was pre-planned. Everyone told me, "People will understand," if I couldn't do it, but I wanted to demonstrate the spiritual backbone a believer has—we can get through anything life brings us to.

Since the rough start of 2020, God has unleashed my leadership and influence in ways I could never have imagined. It is hard to believe, but God took my backbone and gave me a megaphone.

I get to lead leaders. I get to feed leaders. I started a non-profit that exists to encourage, inspire, and empower leaders. I am coaching business leaders and entrepreneurs. And it all started because I had a backbone.

Leader, grow your backbone. Proverbs 24:10 reads, "If you fail under pressure, your strength is too small."

UNLEASH YOUR THOUGHTS

Was 2020 tough? If so, explain how?

_____

_____

_____

_____

_____

_____

_____

_____

_____

_____

_____

What's your why? What keeps you going?

_____

_____

_____

_____

_____

_____

_____

_____

_____

_____

_____

IF YOU DON'T HAVE A BACKBONE YOU SHOULDN'T HAVE A MICROPHONE

Take a moment to pause and reflect. In the midst of some of the losses, where have you seen some wins in your life?

_____

_____

_____

_____

_____

_____

_____

_____

_____

_____

_____

What keeps you on the sidelines?

_____

_____

_____

_____

_____

_____

_____

_____

_____

_____

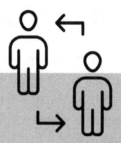

LEADERS ADAPT TO CHANGE

Every great leader has the ability to change. It doesn't mean that you change who you are, but sometimes, you need to adjust how you do who you are! Reread that line again: sometimes, you need to adjust how you do who you are.

> *Sometimes, you need to adjust how you do who you are.*

Several years ago, we had a family in our church that we had become close to, but as the church started to grow, our schedule wasn't as open. While we were leading a church of seventy-five with three staff members, we had a lot of time, but when we were leading a church of a thousand with twenty staff members, we had less. They didn't like that I could not stop everything to just hang out. They started saying to other people, "They are different than they used to be." What was my response? "Thank you because if I am the same leader as five years ago, you need a new leader." I believe in adapting to the opportunities God puts in front of me.

I am not saying anyone needs to change who they are—just adjust how they do who they are! Who you are is who you are, but we do have to be able to control how we do who we are.

Every leader needs to cultivate three qualities of adaptation. First, leaders who adapt have a clear vision. They don't get stuck in the how as much as the what. For the leader, it is the why behind the what. Instead, some leaders get so fixated on what they do that they lose sight of the original mission of their business or organization.

Second, leaders who adapt have an insatiable curiosity. They are always looking to try new things to accomplish their mission. They investigate and experiment. One time, I had a board member tell me, "Pastor, you are constantly changing. If something isn't working, you change it." I then asked a simple question, "How long do you ride a dead horse?" The silence was deafening.

I have this holy curiosity to try anything to help us fulfill our goals as an organization. Every leader needs that same curiosity—that ability to experiment and adjust. If you don't adapt, you will be trapped.

Finally, leaders who adapt are creative geniuses. If something's not working, they will find a way to make it work. My friend Ed Young says, "If something ain't broke, break it." In other words, sometimes you have to force adaption because growth happens at the intersection of discomfort and change. That means you will have to break some things that seem to be going well to keep the main thing from breaking.

Every leader is a creative genius in some way. And creativity is often revealed in the pressure of changing things up or breaking things down.

As I was working on this book, I had a very dear friend and pastor call me. The conversation started like this: "Todd, you have some gifts and talents, but there is one thing that I believe can keep you from reaching your potential." It was a raw and real moment; my wife has told me the same thing for years. But I needed someone else to confirm what she felt. Now, I am already adapting some leadership traits to accommodate that.

UNLEASH YOUR THOUGHTS

What is your vision?

_____

_____

_____

_____

_____

_____

_____

_____

_____

_____

_____

_____

_____

_____

_____

_____

_____

_____

_____

_____

_____

_____

_____

_____

What are some things you need to adapt to make your organization or business better?

_____

_____

_____

_____

_____

_____

_____

_____

_____

_____

_____

_____

_____

_____

_____

_____

_____

_____

_____

_____

_____

_____

FEELINGS ARE REAL, BUT THEY ARE NOT ALWAYS TRUE

FEELINGS ARE REAL, BUT THEY ARE NOT ALWAYS TRUE

One of the most important people in my life, next to my family, is a gentleman by the name of Gary Bruegman. He was the dean of students at the Bible college I attended and has remained a counselor, therapist, and life-long friend. He always says, "Feelings are not right or wrong. They are just feelings." Gary is so right. How you feel about something does not determine whether it is true or not. Yes, the feelings are real, but they do not necessarily reflect reality.

> *How you feel about something does not determine whether it is true or not. Yes, the feelings are real, but they do not necessarily reflect reality.*

As a leader, I've had to learn to manage my feelings. Some days I wake up feeling a certain way, but I feel a different way a few hours later. If I don't manage my feelings, my feelings will end up managing me. That's why I don't make major decisions when I am having an emotional moment. Emotional decisions usually cause commotional collisions. That's why leaders have to manage their emotions.

There are four ways that every leader can master their emotions. First, you have to look within. Stay in touch with your emotions. Examine why you feel the way you do and if your emotions are clouding your judgment. Strong leaders master their internal conversations.

Second, you have to look back. One of the most important tactics of emotional balance is looking into the past—not living in it but learning from it. That is about self-discovery. Your history will help to shape your destiny. So look back.

Every leader should learn the art of journaling. Writing down what you have been through or are going through is a healthy practice, so you have something to look back on. What's not written down is quickly forgotten. If you have forgotten where you've been, you'll never get to where you are headed.

Once you have looked within and taken a look back, you are ready for the next way. Third, you have to look ahead. Your emotions can be kept in check when you realize they can affect your future. Yelling at your boss is much harder when you realize they will probably let you go. Plus, if you don't look ahead, you might make long-term decisions based on short-term emotions. Looking into the future lets you see how the decisions you make today have an impact on tomorrow's outcome. When leaders know they can't fly off the handle, it helps them manage their emotions.

Finally, you have to look up. This is the spiritual component of managing your emotions. For me, I choose to look up to God in prayer, Bible reading, journaling, worship, and meditation. At some point, leaders have to recognize that we need help when it comes to keeping our emotions in control. We cannot do it solely on our own. God is the greatest source of comfort.

Listen to 2 Corinthians 1:3-4:

All praise to God, the Father of our Lord Jesus Christ. God is our merciful Father and the source of all comfort. He comforts us in all our troubles so that we can comfort others. When they are troubled, we will be able to give them the same comfort God has given us.

When you trust in God and lean into Him, He will keep your emotions more balanced and help you lead from an emotionally stable position. This matters to every leader who desires to grow!

UNLEASH YOUR THOUGHTS

Are your feelings usually positive or negative?

_____

_____

_____

_____

_____

_____

_____

_____

_____

_____

How do you express your feelings?

_____

_____

_____

_____

_____

_____

_____

_____

_____

FEELINGS ARE REAL, BUT THEY ARE NOT ALWAYS TRUE

Do you have a journal to take notes or write down your feelings and emotions in? Why or why not?

_____

_____

_____

_____

_____

_____

_____

_____

_____

_____

_____

_____

_____

_____

_____

_____

_____

_____

_____

LEAD WITH GRACE

G race. It is a lost quality of leadership in today's culture. Several years ago, I had a friend go through a moral failure. It was devastating. He was an influential pastor and leader. He decided to submit to his denomination for ministry restoration. He lost his church, many of his friends, and his reputation. On more than one occasion, he was told, "You must feel pain." What? Everything in me wanted to scream, *No, my job is to help remove the pain.* True leaders don't push people to their pain threshold. They actually extend radical grace to the person who needs it.

> *True leaders don't push people to their pain threshold. They actually extend radical grace to the person who needs it.*

Grace is not about justifying someone's behavior. It is about offering that person a third or fourth chance at correcting the wrongs they have done. Yes, even in the workplace. Now, some failures cannot be overlooked, but many can be corrected with kindness and mercy—another two lost characteristics of our culture.

I want to lead with grace because I have been given a lot of grace. That is a fact. I have learned that you never know when the grace you failed to give someone is the grace you'll need from someone else! Choose to live and lead with grace.

Grace is not the ability to look over or past failure but to look through it. To see the good in others that God has seen in you. It seems to me that most leaders lose grace the longer they are leading. They forget about the mishaps of their early leadership days and tend to lead from an old mindset when grace wasn't high on the list of leadership traits.

What does it practically look like to lead with grace? After all, you don't want to look like a doormat to the people you lead. First, leading with grace requires connection over correction. If someone missed a deadline, ask them why before you determine that they have bad time-management skills. Get into their world. Connect with them. It is quite possible they had a family emergency or hit a personal crisis. If your response is correction over connection, you will probably see an incredible turnover of employees every year. Grace gives you the ability to listen to someone's heart before speaking to their lack of execution.

Second, leading with grace requires person over project. Most leaders are so focused on the project they don't care whom they run over to get the project done. My wife, Mary, has taught me over our twenty-plus years of marriage to prioritize people. If you are a get-it-done person, then you are going to have to sometimes—wait for it—hit the pause button in order to take care of your people.

Third, leading with grace requires conversation over condemnation. This is a biggie for leaders. We must be careful not to make a decision without having all of the information. It may be possible that you, as the employer, did not clearly express the deadline or that there was a miscommunication regarding who was taking the lead on the project. A conversation allows you to gather information. Long before you condemn the person's performance, you must talk it through.

The more you lead with grace, the more your leadership will empower your staff. They will feel confident that they can grow with you. Meanwhile, not leading with grace could become a lid to your organization fulfilling its short- and long-term missions.

UNLEASH YOUR THOUGHTS

In what area do you need the most grace?

_____

_____

_____

_____

_____

_____

_____

_____

_____

_____

_____

_____

_____

_____

_____

_____

_____

_____

_____

_____

_____

_____

_____

Have you done more correcting than connecting? Reflect.

_____

_____

_____

_____

_____

_____

_____

_____

_____

_____

_____

_____

_____

_____

_____

_____

_____

_____

_____

_____

_____

_____

_____

_____

LEARN HOW TO TALK TO YOURSELF

Ever since I was a little kid, I've talked to myself. It's true. (Notice that I waited until we were twenty-seven principles in before I told you that.) I used to think I was crazy, but then I read a verse in the Bible. It said, "But David encouraged himself in the LORD his God" (1 Samuel 30:6, KJV). He had to talk himself into some real encouragement. King David, God's anointed one, still needed to do some positive self-talk! Yes, he did, and we need to also.

Most people are great at negative self-talk. We say or think things like, *I am so stupid,* or *What an idiot.* These are sentiments that many leaders repeat often when they miss a deadline or forget a detail. But that negative self-talk gets into a person's spirit, and the more they say it, the more they start to believe it. That's why words matter. Not just the words we speak to others but the words we speak over ourselves.

> *Words matter. Not just the words we speak to others but the words we speak over ourselves.*

So, how do you talk to yourself? You can't walk around the office having conversations with yourself aloud; people will think you are crazy. But there are a few simple ways that you can find some healthy patterns to speak to your inner you. First, replace the negative self-talk with positive declarations. This seems like common sense, but the funny thing about common sense is that it's not that common anymore!

Stop saying you cannot, and start declaring you will. Your life moves in the direction of your lips. That's why you must choose life-giving words.

Wake up every day, walk into the bathroom, and say, "I am the best looking person in here," even if it's just you!

Second, minimize the negative voices in your circle. No, you do not want yes-people in your circle, but you do want *Yes, we can!* people in your life. In fact, you need them. Most people hear more negative voices than positive ones. I grew up in a verbally abusive home. I heard things like, "If I didn't have you, your father would still be here." Imagine hearing that over and over again into adulthood. For a long time, I believed it. Now, I did not remove my mom from my life, but I did minimize her voice in it. Every leader has to make hard decisions about the voices they listen to. This is why it matters: the voices you hear will be the words you repeat to yourself. Minimize the negative voices in your circle.

Third, surround yourself with positive people. I am so grateful for the positive voices God has brought into my life, starting in my own home. As a leader, I've made the hard decision to make sure I am surrounded by life-giving, encouraging people. Every leader needs to be fenced in by positive voices. Those people become an incubator for the leader's self-talk. According to the *Harvard Business Review,* the recommended praise-to-criticism ratio is 5:1, based on an academic study.[5]

---

5 Jack Zenger and Joseph Folkman "The Ideal Praise-to-Criticism Ratio," *Harvard Business Review*, 15 Mar. 2013, https://hbr.org/2013/03/the-ideal-praise-to-criticism.

That means for every criticism, your staff needs five praises. That is true of yourself too.

I would suggest that for every negative person in your life, you will need five positive people to counterbalance the negativity. If you do not have the right people in your life, the words you speak over your life will most likely be negative and self-defeating.

Words matter. That's why the words you say about yourself and to yourself should be encouraging, positive, and uplifting. Don't fall into the quicksand of negative self-talk.

UNLEASH YOUR THOUGHTS

How do you talk to yourself? Are your words negative or positive?

_____

_____

_____

_____

_____

_____

_____

_____

_____

_____

_____

_____

_____

_____

_____

Name five people who are always positive!

_____

_____

_____

_____

_____

LEADERS ARE NOT ALWAYS THE SMARTEST PERSON IN THE ROOM

I have a confession to make. I am not the sharpest tool in the shed, and that is okay. I learned years ago that if I have to be the most brilliant person in any environment, I probably need a new environment. Our surroundings matter to our growth. The more we are around sharp people, the sharper we will become, but we have to be okay with not being the smartest person in the room in every circumstance.

There are people on my team that are sharper than me at certain things. For example, I used to do a lot of video and graphic design in the early years of our church, but now most graphics are done by my son, Malachi, and nearly all of our video projects are done by another member of our team named Steve. They have way more skill and capacity than I do in those areas, and I am totally fine with that. Their being sharper at those things allows me to focus on my priorities. They are my go-tos in the media arena.

Leaders who have to be the best at everything tend to underestimate their team members' contributions. This creates a toxic work environment which causes employees to feel little-to-no value for the work they do or from the people they do it for. When a leader unleashes a team to be smarter than anyone else in their area of expertise, they can watch how that team's joy, competence, and personal investment go up.

Our job as a leader is to hire smarter people than we are in the areas that are not our primary focus or function. Period.

Therefore, our job as a leader is to hire smarter people than we are in the areas that are not our primary focus or function. Period.

It is also a priority for leaders to put themselves in places with other leaders whose skill capacities and abilities are beyond theirs. This is vital because the time we spend with sharp people will make us sharper. The Bible teaches, "As iron sharpens iron, so a friend sharpens a friend" (Proverbs 27:17). In other words, two strong leaders sharpening each other makes you both stronger.

Let me say something that needs to be heard: insecure leaders are always the smartest in the room—at least in their own minds. They hire less competent people, so they appear brilliant. They minimize other people's ideas. They find ways to showcase themselves instead of celebrating others.

I have not always been a strong leader. In my early years, I was very insecure. However, as I became confident in myself, I became less intimidated by the people around me. I have a great staff member. His name is Matt, he has been on our team a long time, and he is a better people person than me. He loves to be around people. Me, I love people, but I don't *have* to be around them. He *needs* people around him. That used to bother me. Now I realize it frees me to be me and him to do what he loves. It's a good balance.

Brigette Hyacinth, author of *Leading the Workforce of the Future*, stated the following in a 2019 article:

LEADERS ARE NOT ALWAYS THE SMARTEST PERSON IN THE ROOM

With advances in technology and unprecedented levels of change, leaders will need to hire people who are smarter than they are, and draw on the diversity and expertise of everyone in the room. This can be the difference between success and failure.[6]

Everyone has something of value to add. The best of leaders know how to surround themselves with greatness and still be great too. Unleash your leadership and surround yourself with some incredibly gifted, talented, and sharp people.

6 Brigette Hyacinth, "Good Leaders Don't Try to Be the Smartest Person in the Room," *LinkedIn*, 9 July 2019, https://se.linkedin.com/pulse/good-leaders-dont-try-smartest-person-room-brigette-hyacinth?trk=portfolio_article_card_title.

UNLEASH YOUR THOUGHTS

Whom can you delegate to or empower that might be better than you in a certain area?

_____

_____

_____

_____

_____

_____

_____

_____

Do you need to surround yourself with other leaders who are better than you?

_____

_____

_____

_____

_____

_____

_____

_____

_____

_____

YOU CAPTURE THE ANOINTING OF THOSE YOU ARE AROUND

YOU CAPTURE THE ANOINTING OF THOSE YOU ARE AROUND

The Bible declares, "Walk with the wise and become wise; associate with fools and get in trouble" (Proverbs 13:20). In other words, you capture the anointing of those you are around! That's why you have to limit your time with certain people and, yes, even certain leaders. Not every person deserves your time. While bad habits and bad attitudes will try to sink your leadership if you spend time with the wrong people, people with good habits and good attitudes will lift you to their level.

> *While bad habits and bad attitudes will try to sink your leadership if you spend time with the wrong people, people with good habits and good attitudes will lift you to their level.*

I have said for years, "Show me your friends, and I will show you your future." Get around the right people! If you want a happy marriage, do not hang around your twenty divorced friends. If you want to be better with money, stop partying with the broke. If you want to be a better pastor, get around better pastors. If you want to be a stronger CEO, call another successful CEO, and take them out to lunch. You will capture the good or bad from the people you associate with.

The best of leaders rub shoulders with better leaders. Mary and I are very cautious about whom we spend time with. We say no to a lot of invites, not because we don't love people, but because we have to be wise in where we spend our time.

All it takes is one toxic relationship to contaminate a family, a job, a group of friends, or even a church. We have seen it time and time again. We want to capture the right anointing!

Don't blame a clown for acting like a clown—just stop going to their circus. That's great advice for any leader. At some point in your leadership, you have to consciously choose what you want to capture.

Several years ago, Mary and I were introduced to David and Nicole Crank. They pastor Faith Church in St. Louis, Missouri, and West Palm Beach, Florida. There was something magnetic about them. We followed them on social media for years. All of a sudden, God opened a door for us. We were blown away by how willing they were to open their lives to us. Before they became pastors, they were highly successful businesspeople. God has blessed them in many ways, and the closer we've gotten to them—the more we've gotten to know them—the more we've begun to capture some of their anointing.

That one relationship has catapulted us to another level. Things we never thought we could achieve, we are now pursuing. God has begun to open up doors, relationships, and opportunities because we captured a little bit of what they have. Someone once said, "A person's mind is like a rubber band. Once stretched, it never goes back to what it was." That's the essence of capturing the anointing. You are stretched, and you experience growth at levels you could never imagine.

YOU CAPTURE THE ANOINTING OF THOSE YOU ARE AROUND

Whom you hang with will ultimately determine how high you can go. That means, as a leader, you will have to be cautious about who you allow into your life because you will catch what they've got. I give time to everybody, but I spend time with the right people. After all, friends are like elevators; they either take you up or bring you down.

Your time is a valuable resource. Invest it wisely, and become wise. Spend the most time with the people you want to be most like, and before you know it, you will have to introduce yourself to yourself because you will be a new, better leader.

UNLEASH YOUR THOUGHTS

Which anointed business owners, leaders, and great people can you surround yourself with?

_____

_____

_____

_____

_____

_____

_____

_____

_____

Are the people you surround yourself with growing you or stunting you?

_____

_____

_____

_____

_____

_____

_____

_____

_____

_____

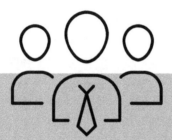

LEADERSHIP: YOU EITHER HAVE IT OR YOU FAKE IT

Have you ever asked yourself, *Why does ___ seem to always be successful?* I firmly believe a person's success is determined by their leadership competence. As John C. Maxwell has said, "Leadership is influence, nothing more, nothing less."[7] I really do believe that you've either got the gift of leadership, or you don't.

Everyone leads something. A parent leads their home. A coach leads their team. An entrepreneur leads their business. A pastor leads their church. However, there are many people today who lead but do not have the gift of leadership. It is possible to learn some leadership principles that will help you as a leader, but the most successful of leaders have a gift to lead.

However, if you don't feel like you have it, all is not lost. The Bible declares, "If God has given you leadership ability, take the responsibility seriously" (Romans 12:8). Notice the "If God." That means not everyone is given the spiritual gift of leadership. This does not mean you can't lead if you don't have the spiritual gift, but if you have the spiritual gift, leadership will come more naturally to you.

> *If you have no one following you somewhere, then you are probably not leading anything because the greatest indicator of one's leadership is buy-in.*

---

7 The John Maxwell Company, "7 Factors That Influence Influence," *John Maxwell*, 8 July 2013, https://www.johnmaxwell.com/blog/7-factors-that-influence-influence/.

Leaders always have followers. If you have no one following you somewhere, then you are probably not leading anything because the greatest indicator of one's leadership is buy-in. The strongest of leaders can get people to buy into their vision. But leaders in title only—those without the gift—have potential to create a stranglehold in any organization or business because their followers don't buy into the dream.

So what do you do if you don't have the gift of leadership? It's pretty simple: surround yourself with people that do. Learn their practices, develop their habits, and replicate their principles. You can learn leadership by watching and imitating others. The apostle Paul said, "And you should imitate me, just as I imitate Christ" (1 Corinthians 11:1). Paul was teaching the church in Corinth: if you don't know what to do, just do what I do. Leaders who don't have the gift must imitate those that do. Before you know it, it will become second nature.

If you have the gift of leadership, you probably already know it. The question really is, "What are you going to do with it?" Those who seem to have natural leadership ability can be seen on the football field, on the basketball court, or in the boardroom. They just naturally rise to the top. Natural leaders shouldn't get cocky or prideful. They should remain humble in the process of God's elevation for their life.

Leadership is a gift of God; titles are given by people. When those two collide, there will be an elevation of your influence and impact on the people surrounding your life. Every leader needs to recognize, walk in, and embrace their unique calling to lead—no matter what level their leadership is.

So, I guess what I am saying is that leaders are both born and made. No matter which side you fall on, you can walk in confidence knowing that God "who began the good work within you, will continue his work until it is finally finished on the day when Christ Jesus returns" (Philippians 1:6). You are a leader in progress.

Keep going. Keep growing.

UNLEASH YOUR THOUGHTS

Do you have the gift of leadership? How can you tell?

_____

_____

_____

_____

_____

_____

_____

_____

_____

_____

From whom or where can you learn?

_____

_____

_____

_____

_____

_____

_____

_____

_____

_____

What leadership podcast can you listen to? What books can you read?

_____

_____

_____

_____

_____

_____

_____

_____

_____

_____

_____

_____

_____

_____

_____

_____

_____

WHEN YOU COMPLAIN YOU REMAIN

We tell our kids all the time, "When you complain, you remain." Complaining keeps you where you are instead of where you want to be. Leaders who get comfortable with complaining will settle in the valley of mediocrity. Someone once said, "Happiness comes a lot easier when you stop complaining about your problems and start being grateful for all the problems you don't have." If your focus is on your negative circumstances, you will always struggle with joy, peace, vision, and, yes, even your leadership.

> *Leaders who get comfortable with complaining will settle in the valley of mediocrity.*

The Bible instructs, "Do everything without complaining and arguing" (Philippians 2:14). That's why you have to stay away from certain "still" people: still broke, still complaining, still hating, still cheating, still lying, and still nowhere. As leaders, we have to set a higher standard.

As a pastor, one of the strangest things I encounter is a pastor who complains about their staff or the people they lead. It's often hard to hear because they are complaining about the very people they hired and the ones God called them to lead. This actually means that they are complaining about their calling. And leaders that complain remain.

The easiest way to protect yourself from complaining is to lead from a grateful heart. Lead with an attitude of gratitude.

Stay focused on what God is doing. Celebrate the good times and the challenging ones. Refuse to allow yourself to be caught in the prison of irritability. Rise above it.

In the Bible, it was a spirit of complaining that kept the children of Israel wandering in the wilderness for forty years. And that same complaining heart can keep you from your leadership-promised land too.

Terry Joseph Busch, in an article titled "Are You the Leader Who Complains Too Much?"[8] shared five questions to reveal if you are an obsessive complainer:

1. When a colleague sees you at their door or cubicle, do they take a deep breath as if to say, "What now?"
2. Are they slow to return your calls or emails?
3. Do they listen for a few polite minutes and then have to go to an appointment or take another call?
4. Do they vent to you, or are you always the venter and never the ventee?
5. Do you reject all constructive suggestions for solving the issue you are complaining about? Are you complaining about the same thing now that you did six months ago?

These are gut-wrenching questions that every leader needs to ask to reveal whether or not they have become a complaining leader.

---

8 Terry Joseph Busch, "Are You the Leader Who Complains Too Much?" *SHRM*, 1 Apr. 2014, https://www.shrm.org/hr-today/news/hr-magazine/pages/0414-excessive-complaining.aspx.

Here's the devastating truth: no one wants to follow a leader that complains. As the leader goes, so goes the organization and everyone they lead! Whining, complaining, and grumbling will keep us from our potential as leaders.

Let me be honest. There are many times I catch myself in the clutches of complaining, and I have to refocus my way out of it. If I stay there too long, it'll be really hard to bounce out of the complaining. We can break the back of complaining by celebrating all that is happening around, in, and through us. That's what unleashed leaders do!

UNLEASH YOUR THOUGHTS

Do you complain, or are you grateful?

_____

_____

_____

_____

_____

Why do you complain? Do you complain about your job, calling, or the people you lead?

_____

_____

_____

_____

_____

_____

_____

_____

_____

_____

_____

_____

_____

BAD LEADERS TEACH AS MUCH AS GOOD LEADERS

BAD LEADERS TEACH AS MUCH AS GOOD LEADERS

Have you ever worked for a bad leader? I have. After graduating from Bible college, I put ministry on hold because I could not get a job as a single youth pastor. I worked at an insurance company as a telemarketer, making cold calls in hopes of generating leads for the agents. I started just working for one agent, but soon it became two. A third agent was selling long-term care insurance, and he wanted me on his team. He pulled me aside one day and said, "I'll give you 10 percent of every cold call that turns into a sale."

I was like, "Yeah, let's go."

About a month in, I found out that was not legal. I could not take a percentage of any commission because I was not a licensed insurance agent. I was called into his boss's office and told I could no longer do that. I apologized and let them know I had no idea. They kept us both on because we were so good. Meanwhile, he approached me privately after the meeting and said, "I'll just cut you a check from my earnings, and it will be our secret."

I politely said, "No, thank you. I am a Christian, and that would be dishonest."

He pushed. I left his office and went to his supervisor. I resigned, and he was fired.

I learned something very important in the eighteen months I worked there. My integrity mattered more than a job. I learned that from an individual who had zero integrity. After that experience, I made a commitment to be real and transparent no matter what position I held.

> *You can learn from anybody—even bad leaders. In fact, bad leaders are often better teachers because they don't even know they are teaching you!*

If you are older, you'll remember the crash test dummies commercial. If not, YouTube it. It's too much to explain, but the final piece of the commercial was the slogan, "You can learn a lot from a dummy." That is 100 percent true. You can learn from anybody—even bad leaders. In fact, bad leaders are often better teachers because they don't even know they are teaching you! Grab every lesson you can from anywhere you can, so you don't make their mistakes.

So, how do you work under a bad leader? I believe there are four keys that will help you unleash your leadership even if you are serving under a poor leader:

1. Recognize they won't be there long. Decide to serve with excellence and commitment. Let God make the adjustments as He sees fit.

2. Understand that a bad leader will make good leaders shine. Your leadership will grow in the middle of serving under a bad leader. I have seen that in my own life. Keep doing what is right because it's right, and everything will turn out right.

3. If a bad leader is trying to contaminate you, then go to their supervisor (after you have asked them to

self-correct). If that leader becomes toxic to your leadership, you have a responsibility to the business to get things corrected.

4. Ask God for wisdom. These are not easy decisions or discussions, but they are necessary. The only person who will give you the correct next steps or words is God. Ask Him for help.

Bad leaders teach you what not to do. If you can recognize the importance of learning from everybody, you will be able to advance in every environment—even the negative ones!

UNLEASH YOUR THOUGHTS

You can learn from anybody—even bad leaders. What lessons have you grabbed from the mistakes of a bad leader?

_____

_____

_____

_____

_____

_____

_____

_____

_____

How has your leadership shone while serving under a bad leader?

_____

_____

_____

_____

_____

_____

_____

_____

_____

_____

In what ways are you serving with excellence and commitment? Are you allowing God to make the adjustments?

_____

_____

_____

_____

_____

_____

_____

_____

_____

_____

_____

_____

_____

_____

_____

_____

_____

_____

_____

_____

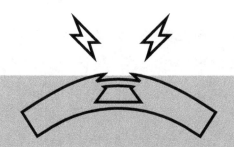

LEADERS MUST TAKE A BREAK OR THEY WILL BREAK

One of the most difficult things a leader must do is learn how to take a break, a vacation, or a sabbath. No matter what you call it, every leader needs time to refresh and re-energize. No leader can run on empty forever. At some point, leaders must recognize when they are nearing their breaking point. If they do not, they will eventually break.

> *One of the biggest reasons senior leaders do not want to go away is because they are worried everything will fall apart in their absence. If you cannot get away, you are doing something wrong.*

One of the biggest reasons senior leaders do not want to go away is because they are worried everything will fall apart in their absence. If that were the case, it would reveal *failed* leadership—not *absent* leadership. If you cannot get away, you are doing something wrong. Even the top 1 percent of leaders make time to vacation or rest. Let me give you five reasons why I believe every leader must learn how to and even force themselves to take breaks.

First, creativity flows from a place of pause. Most of my greatest ideas have come to mind while I was on a vacation, sabbatical, or getaway. I find that creativity is best seen in the pause. It happens when you are out of the rhythm of routine. Take a break and watch your creativity flourish.

Second, it will improve your trust in your leadership. When you return to the office from an extended absence, you will see how good (or bad) you are doing as a leader. Did the team execute without you? That is not a question that reveals your team doesn't need you. It actually shows that you have done your job as a leader. The better your team did, the better you have led them.

Third, it allows others to lead. This is critical. If you are the only one who can lead, then you have hit your limit as a leader, but as you empower others, even in your absence, they pick up the mantle of leadership. Now, this is not where people assume leadership. After all, leadership is a leader's to give, not an employee's to take. So, make sure you are very clear on delegation. Go away, and celebrate the fact that the others are able to lead. Trust me. As this happens, you will take more time off—not less.

Fourth, it protects your health. Every leader needs to take a break. This is vital to your physical and mental health. Rest and sleep play an important role in your overall health but especially your immune system. If you are constantly running, running, running, but not resting, resting, resting, your body will eventually send signals—exhaustion, weakness, lethargy, and more. Take time to rest; it will help you last even longer in leadership.

Fifth, it allows your organization to grow faster. One of the biggest complaints I hear from leaders is that their bench is not deep enough. Being absent allows you to work on your second- and third-level leaders. Give them some extra work or responsibility when you go away, and see if they can rise to it. If they do, this will cause exponential growth for your business, church, or nonprofit.

Those are the benefits. But what happens if you don't take a break? You will break, but even more, the organization you spent a lifetime building will break alongside you. So, for the health of it, take a break and watch your leadership influence grow more and more.

Take a break, or you will break.

UNLEASH YOUR THOUGHTS

Why is it difficult for you to take a break, vacation, or a sabbath?

_____

_____

_____

_____

_____

_____

_____

_____

_____

_____

Creativity is best seen in the pause. How can you break the rhythm of routine to see your creativity?

_____

_____

_____

_____

_____

_____

_____

_____

_____

_____

LEADERS MUST TAKE A BREAK OR THEY WILL BREAK

Which area of your life is suffering the most when you are on the go, go, go? Physical? Emotional? Mental? Spiritual?

_____

_____

_____

_____

_____

_____

_____

_____

_____

_____

Write down how you can take some time to refresh and re-energize.

_____

_____

_____

_____

_____

_____

_____

_____

_____

_____

_____

REFUSE TO GET STUCK IN THE COMPARATIVE NARRATIVE

Comparison is one of the most debilitating traits of a leader. It keeps us from celebrating all of the great things we have done because they're compared to the even greater things others have done. The Bible declares in 2 Corinthians 10:12:

> Oh, don't worry; we wouldn't dare say that we are as wonderful as these other men who tell you how important they are! But they are only comparing themselves with each other, using themselves as the standard of measurement. How ignorant.

Basically, the Bible is calling the trait of comparison foolishness. It's a waste of time. God did not call you to be anyone else. He called you to be you.

> *The Bible calls the trait of comparison foolishness. It's a waste of time. God did not call you to be anyone else. He called you to be you.*

One of the most freeing things I have ever discovered in leadership is that nobody can beat me at being me! That's 100 percent true. When God made you, He broke the mold. Too many leaders want to replicate and duplicate, instead of originate. You are one of a kind. That means you have to refuse to get stuck in the comparative narrative.

Unhealthy comparison leads to unholy competition. There is nothing wrong with learning from others or utilizing some basic principles of their leadership. However, when you start to compare every detail to what, how, or why "they" do it, you create unholy competition.

I used to get stuck comparing my leadership, my preaching, or my style to other pastors. That left me feeling less than, worse off, or even illegitimate. Today, I choose to just be me because nobody can beat me at that.

Someone will always be better at what you do. That's just a fact, but it cannot be your motivation. Great leaders are not motivated by other people's abilities; they are motivated by their personal and corporate missions.

Comparison is like going in circles. You are moving, but you are not going anywhere. If you are in the circle of comparison, at some point, you are going to have to break that cycle.

Henna Inam, in her article "Comparison Is the Enemy of Leadership," suggests our comparison of others evokes one of the following responses:

- We find ourselves inferior to them.
- We find ourselves superior to them.
- We make them the frame through which we see ourselves.[9]

How true are those? Comparison is a trap that will keep us from our God-given destinies because we are framing our leadership through other people instead of the God who gave us our positions or titles.

---

9 Henna Inam, "Comparison Is the Enemy of Leadership," *Transformational Leadership*, 1 Nov. 2018, https://transformleaders.tv/comparison-is-the-enemy-of-leadership/.

REFUSE TO GET STUCK IN THE COMPARATIVE NARRATIVE

If you enjoy watching the NBA draft, they will always compare the draftee to a former or current elite NBA player. The same thing happens in every sport. Why? Because it's in our nature to compare. Therefore, we have to resist the urge even when we want to. Great leaders fight off the need to compare because they know that when people compare, they despair.

Nobody can beat you at being you, so be the best you that you can be! The only comparison you should make is whether or not you are walking in your leadership gifts, abilities, and callings. Now, get out there, and be the best version of yourself! Start today.

UNLEASH YOUR THOUGHTS

When have you allowed comparison to keep you from your God-given destiny?

_____

_____

_____

_____

_____

_____

_____

_____

_____

_____

_____

Out of the three responses to comparing yourself to others, which one describes you the most?

_____

_____

_____

_____

_____

_____

_____

_____

No one can beat you at being you! Write down how you are walking in your gifting, abilities, and calling!

_____

_____

_____

_____

_____

_____

_____

_____

_____

_____

_____

_____

_____

_____

_____

_____

_____

_____

_____

_____

CRISIS EXAGGERATES THINGS

Every leader knows that when things are going really well, other things can be overlooked and ignored, and most people won't realize it. But when crisis comes, everything gets magnified and exaggerated. One crisis becomes "the sky is falling"—even though it is not.

In 2015, the World Economic Forum reported, "A startling 86 percent of respondents to the Survey on the Global Agenda agree that we have a leadership crisis in the world today."[10] That was in 2015. Imagine what that survey would reveal today! The largest crisis we have is actually how leaders handle crises! A leader who does not have the capacity to manage a crisis will be reduced to managing nothing.

> *A leader who does not have the capacity to manage a crisis will be reduced to managing nothing.*

Crisis exaggerates things, but it also reveals things. That's why in the middle of the challenges of work, business, and corporate growth, we cannot fall into a leadership crisis. We must still be able to manage our people and our purpose in the middle of every difficulty we face.

Every leader will face a financial crisis. When the profits are up, or the tithes are good, everything is good. But what happens when you face a bad quarter or lost income? I've learned

10 Shiza Shahid, "Trend 3. Lack of Leadership," *Outlook on the Global Agenda 2015*, https://reports.weforum.org/outlook-global-agenda-2015/top-10-trends-of-2015/3-lack-of-leadership/?doing_wp_cron=1541243910.4283349514007568359375.

that the problem with money is money. You either have it, or you don't. When you have it, there is no need to worry about how you will pay your staff—until you don't. Or you invest it in R&D or marketing only to realize your team frivolously spent it. No matter how good a leader is, there will be a season when they face a financial crisis.

Every leader will face the crisis of staffing. Managing, hiring, or firing staff can be one of the most stressful things that we do. Dealing with people is challenging enough. Keeping those individuals on mission is an even greater task. Great leaders hire the wrong people and fire the right people. Why? Because we are human. It's an area of crisis every leader will experience—staffing issues.

Every leader will face the crisis of communication. As someone who has his hand in marketing, I learned years ago that you cannot over-communicate. The two most famous women in the world are Miss Communication and Miss Understanding. Yes, every leader will need to manage them, or things will always look worse. Andy Stanley has said, "Vision leaks." That simply means I have to communicate, communicate, communicate. When I think I have done it well, I need to do it again.

Every leader will face the crisis of change. Change in life is inevitable. Change in leadership is too. Things are changing at the speed of yesterday. Technological advances and social media influence have created immediate change—most of which is probably not healthy, but we won't know that for years. In leadership, I have discovered if someone is unwilling to change, they will become unable to lead. Change is not a crisis to be avoided.

If a leader can navigate crisis, they will be able to lead well and long because crisis exaggerates everything. Under the microscope of pressure, everything is worse than it really is. Leaders will never be able to remove problems, but they must learn to manage them. It's one of the most important traits of a leader. After all, if we can't lead through crisis, then crisis will lead us out of our positions.

UNLEASH YOUR THOUGHTS

A crisis comes, and everything gets magnified and exaggerated! When have you seen this revealed?

_____

_____

_____

_____

_____

_____

_____

_____

_____

_____

How can you better handle a crisis when it comes your way?

_____

_____

_____

_____

_____

_____

_____

_____

_____

_____

CRISIS EXAGGERATES THINGS

How have you managed your calling during times of crisis? How have you managed people?

_____

_____

_____

_____

_____

_____

_____

_____

_____

_____

_____

_____

_____

_____

_____

_____

_____

_____

_____

_____

THINK LIKE YOU DON'T HAVE MONEY

THINK LIKE YOU DON'T HAVE MONEY

I grew up poor. My mom had to work very hard to provide for her three boys. She stretched money in ways I have yet to master. She was brilliant at stretching food, finances, and even memories. I learned a lot from watching her. She was a single mom who didn't have money and yet seemed to have everything. I learned early in life to think like I didn't have money—because I didn't.

Now, things are different! I am not wealthy, but I am blessed. The only thing that has remained with me is that I still think as if I don't have money. I am frugal, thrifty, or cheap—whatever you want to call it. I like finding deals, haggling over prices, or negotiating terms. I don't like to pay full price for anything. And it's not just limited to my home but also to my church.

Personally, I have a beautiful home with an incredible family. We have that because we don't spend money on things that add little-to-no value. We focus on what will bring the greatest return, and that's where we drop the cash.

As a pastor, leader, and manager, I lead our church the same way. I spend money on the things that will yield the greatest spiritual return for our church family. I find ways to negotiate lower prices. I have negotiated three building purchases over the last fifteen years. The first building we purchased was 74 percent off its actual value. The second and third buildings were both 32 percent discounted from their actual value. Some people believe God has given me a "building anointing" or the ability to acquire buildings at reduced prices. I just still think like I have no money!

> *It does not matter if you are in a for-profit business or a nonprofit organization. Every leader has to answer for every dollar spent, invested, or wasted.*

Leaders have to save money anywhere and everywhere. Budgets matter! Bottom lines matter! It does not matter if you are in a for-profit business or a nonprofit organization. Every leader has to answer for every dollar spent, invested, or wasted.

Thinking like you have no money forces you to be more creative. I am a creative person, and when I communicate publicly, I use props—almost every time. I created a prop room in our church (it's now grown to two). When I get an idea for a talk or sermon, my first thought is, *Do we have something in the prop room?* If we do, I just saved money. If we don't, we have to shop around to find something. But, as a leader, my first instinct is to think like I have no money to shop with.

Money is a motor, but it is not a motivator. The moment money becomes my motivator, my engine will seize because we don't have unlimited access to cash. Money just helps us accomplish our purpose or vision. But as the CEO or president of an organization, I am responsible for how we spend the resources we have been given.

God has blessed our church with multiple properties and money in the bank, but I still lead like we have no money.

That deposit my mother invested in this little boy is paying dividends of leadership today. She may never have known this side of eternity, but that lesson has helped me become more successful.

Stingy is sacred. Cheap is carnal.

Manage what you've got like you don't have much! It will multiply.

UNLEASH YOUR THOUGHTS

What have you focused on that brings the greatest return, and where have you dropped some cash?

_____

_____

_____

_____

_____

_____

_____

_____

_____

_____

What can you do to change your spending habits?

_____

_____

_____

_____

_____

_____

_____

_____

_____

_____

Is what you are spending on helping to accomplish the purpose of the vision?

_____
_____
_____
_____
_____
_____
_____
_____
_____
_____
_____
_____
_____
_____
_____
_____
_____

LEADERS SEE WHAT OTHERS DO NOT

H elen Keller said, "The only thing worse than being blind is having sight but no vision." Leaders have the capacity to see what other people do not. I am not sure if it's hardwired into their psyches, but I know that unleashed leaders have a vision for detail that is more acute than anyone else on the team.

> *I am not sure if it's hard-wired into their psyches, but I know that unleashed leaders have a vision for detail that is more acute than anyone else on the team.*

I am slightly OCD. It's true. In our church, all the chairs must be perfectly straight! If I am speaking, and they are not lined up right, it bothers me. I see things most people won't. I'll notice the stain on the wall, the chip in the paint, or the person missing from their usual seat. Leaders always see what others do not.

A leader has a unique set of eyes. The great LeRoy Eims wrote, "A leader is one who sees more than others see, who sees farther than others see, and who sees before others do."[11] Just like Walt Disney saw "Disney" for what it was going to be before anyone else saw it we, as leaders, need to see our business, organization, or church for what it could be. Leaders must have wide eyes!

---

11 Don McMinn, "Followers: Leaders 'See' Things Other People Don't See, so Sometimes You Must Simply Trust Your Leader and Follow," *DonMcMinn*, 3 Aug. 2019, https://donmcminn. com/2019/07/followers-leaders-see-things-other-people-dont-see-so-sometimes-you-must-simply-trust-your-leader-and-follow/#.

One of my favorite movies of all time is *ROCKY*. Yes, Rocky! There is nothing like a Sylvester Stallone movie. Sylvester Stallone was reportedly rejected 1,500 times before someone snagged the opportunity he presented. James Dyson created 5,126 prototypes of his vacuum cleaner before he created the one. What do both of these leaders have in common? They saw what others did not. They looked beyond obstacles to see opportunities!

At some point, every leader is going to have to develop a set of eyes that see things others don't and beyond what others do! It's a leader's vision that sets them apart from every other person on the planet. Leaders need to see before others and beyond others. They must see what others cannot.

Author and blogger Don McMinn describes that visual acuity perfectly:

Bill Gates saw a computer on every desk; Sam Walton saw a chain of discount retail stores; Steve Jobs saw a handheld device that would function as a phone and a link to the world; President Kennedy visualized an American going to the moon and returning; President Eisenhower saw an interstate highway system, much like the German autobahn that he saw during the war; the apostle Paul saw the church, a spiritual community of believers.

If you want to unleash your leadership, you have to have leader-vision. What's leader-vision? It's kind of like super-vision, but it's the vision a leader has to see before and beyond what others see. This is critical at any stage. A leader who does not possess it will not be able to lead for very long.

How do you develop a leader-vision?

- Walk in your calling.
- Ask God for the ability to see.
- When you see something, say something.
- Raise up others who see what you see.
- Do something about what you see.

A leader without vision is a leader no one will follow. Hone your leader-vision today. The prophet Habakkuk wrote, "Write my answer plainly on tablets, so that a runner can carry the correct message to others" (Habakkuk 2:2).

In order to make your vision clear, you have to first be able to see!

UNLEASH YOUR THOUGHTS

How do you lead with unique, wide eyes as an unleashed leader?

_____

_____

_____

_____

_____

_____

_____

_____

_____

In what ways does your vision set you apart from those you lead?

_____

_____

_____

_____

_____

_____

_____

_____

_____

How are you developing your leader-vision?

_____

_____

_____

_____

_____

_____

_____

_____

_____

_____

_____

_____

_____

_____

_____

_____

_____

_____

_____

_____

_____

_____

_____

DON'T LET YOUR SYSTEM BECOME YOUR STRANGLE

Everyone has used the acronym for system: **S**ave **Y**our **S**taff **T**ime, **E**nergy, and **M**oney. But many times, we become imprisoned by outdated systems. Systems were never designed to be life-long handcuffs. Many leaders are using systems from thirty years ago, expecting modern-day results. Here's my advice: don't let a system get a stranglehold on you.

> *Many leaders are using systems from thirty years ago, expecting modern-day results. Here's my advice: don't let a system get a stranglehold on you.*

Systems are not eternal. Don't make something that is not eternal, eternal. It will end up crushing your growth and strangling your business potential. Systems that worked for your company as a start-up may not work as a small business. And those systems that work for a small business may not work in a Fortune 500 company.

When is it time to change a system? First, a business must adjust its systems when it outgrows the system. Seems simple, but most people get married to a system. My leadership style is more about being married to our purpose. Our goals, mission, and purpose hardly change, but the systems that support them must change as our organizations grow!

Second, a business must adjust its systems when deficiency outweighs efficiency—when they are no longer productive. Some businesses would rather close than change their systems. "We have always done it this way," is the statement of failing leadership. A leader has the unique responsibility of growing with the company. That growth should cause them to see when a system is deficient.

Third, a business must adjust its systems when the past outpaces the future. Many enterprises that get stuck in what *was* fail to see what *can be*. Most times, this is due to a system failure. I learned years ago that the system you create will give you what the system is designed for. But if your business, church, or organization starts to decline, the first things to check are the systems! When your numbers on all sides start shrinking, it may not be a staffing issue. It may be a systems issue.

When a system is malfunctioning, we cannot wait too long to make adjustments. The longer we wait, the harder it will be to correct, adjust, tweak, and change. Ed Young says, "Small tweaks take you to higher peaks." Some systems require small adjustments. Others are going to take some hard work and deep thought.

There are two ways to diagnose your systems: self-diagnose or get some help. The top 1 percent of leaders can usually self-diagnose. The rest of us will need to get some help in seeing our organization from a different perspective. Hiring a coach or consultant may be what's required, but you can also get some 1-percent people in your circle to speak into your leadership. I do both! I don't want to be the clog in my leadership pipeline! Strong leaders do whatever it takes for however long it takes to get to the right solution.

Don't panic when your systems are not running at optimal levels. Don't abandon ship. Just evaluate your systems, and do it right away.

UNLEASH YOUR THOUGHTS

Has there been a system clog with you as a leader? Where?

_____

_____

_____

_____

_____

_____

_____

_____

_____

_____

_____

What can you do to clear a clogged system?

_____

_____

_____

_____

_____

_____

_____

_____

_____

_____

Do you need to diagnose your system through a coach or consultant?

_____

_____

_____

_____

_____

_____

_____

_____

_____

_____

THE ART OF THE NEXT QUESTION

Have you ever heard this statement: "There are a lot of people who are not happy with your decision!" or something like that? Most leaders hear that question and immediately react. I have developed something over the years that I call "the art of the next question." If I had a staff member tell me the above statement, I would respond with, "How many?" I would let them answer. Then I would ask, "Who?" Typically that "there are a lot" comes down to only three or even fewer.

Many leaders fail to ask the next question in order to get the right information. Imagine me thinking there are a lot of people unhappy with my decision when there is only one. That's a huge difference. One of the most important things you can do, then, when it comes to information, is manage the art of the next question. Trust me. It'll save you a lot of misinformation.

> *One of the most important things you can do when it comes to information is manage the art of the next question.*

Asking questions is really a part of leadership. The best of leaders are always on a quest for information, and one of the greatest detail collectors is questions. One question can lead to a deep, engaging, and informative conversation.

There are a lot of leadership blogs, articles, and books on asking the right questions, but very few address this idea of the *next* question. You see, to be an unleashed leader, you have to master the art of the *next* question. It will lead you to the answers you need in order to have the right responses or make the correct decisions. Questions are part of life; make them part of your leadership.

Why is the art of the next question so vital? First, it allows you access to additional information. You cannot make decisions until you have all the necessary information. Therefore, you keep asking the next question until you get all of the answers you need.

I have many staff members come to me with information, but it's not enough. I look at them, and they respond, "I should have asked the next question."

My response is always, "Yep."

Second, the art of the next question reveals information about the individual bringing you information. It's not just the content you are evaluating. You are looking into the carrier to see if they have leadership potential or if they're just a task completer. The person who always fails to ask the next question is just a doer, but the person who is growing in their capacity to ask the next question reveals their leadership capability. In our culture, if a person does not ask the next question, they will not be elevated in our organization. It just shows a lack of leadership proficiency.

Finally, the art of the next question allows you to see in more detail what is happening below the surface. In leadership and in life, detail matters! Some people and even some staff can cover things up, but when you keep pounding next question after next question, it is easier to see what's being hidden. You may discover hidden agendas, beliefs, or personal projects. Below the surface is where deep truth lies.

Questions are part of leadership, but most leaders don't ask enough of them. These questions will annoy employees, but they will reveal your leaders. Master the art of the next question, and watch your leadership rise to another level.

UNLEASH YOUR THOUGHTS

When have you found yourself reacting to statements rather than asking the next question?

_____

_____

_____

_____

_____

_____

_____

_____

_____

How can you grow in this area of leadership?

_____

_____

_____

_____

_____

_____

_____

_____

_____

_____

Be honest: are you covering things up to avoid the next question?

_____

_____

_____

_____

_____

_____

_____

_____

_____

_____

Is there someone of whom you need to ask more questions in order to get the job done?

_____

_____

_____

_____

_____

_____

_____

_____

_____

_____

_____

MASTER THE FIRST 120 MINUTES OF YOUR DAY

How you start your day will typically determine how your day goes. That's why it is so important to master the first 120 minutes of your day. Almost every study has concluded that the most successful individuals in leadership wake up between 5:00 a.m. and 6:00 a.m.. Oprah Winfrey revealed to *Parade* magazine that she would wake up at 6:00 a.m. and be to the office by 6:30 a.m. to set her agenda for the day. You see, it's not just about waking up early; it's about waking up with purpose.

> *How you start your day will typically determine how your day goes! Therefore, you need to master the first 120 minutes of your day.*

I typically wake up to start my day at about 5:30 a.m. I take a shower, get dressed, and then spend some time in prayer, reflection, Bible reading, and journaling. After all of that pre-day preparation, I eat breakfast. Then, a few times a week, I will take a walk. It's good exercise for the body and the mind. I come back and start my work day from home. I am not available until I complete my start-up regimen. It frustrates some people, but it helps me be better at what I do.

Let me give you some morning habits that will help you become more efficient and productive for your life of leadership. First, wake up at the same time every day. Break out of the sleeping-in-multiple-times-a-week habit. Get to bed early enough to stay consistent. This helps your body find a healthy rhythm.

Second, do what matters most first. Start your day doing the most important things. For me, that's my spiritual routine. It centers me for the rest of the day. You will have to figure out what works for you, but set your priority around the right focuses.

Third, avoid the unimportant and irrelevant. This is so tough, but limit your social media time. Argh, this is so tough! But social media is a distraction from more successful moments. Avoid the news spin cycle—it's the same thing over and over again. Anything that distracts you from mastering the first 120 minutes of your day should be avoided.

Fourth, don't call or text people until after your first 120 minutes. Trust me. While you are up prepping for your day, most people are sleeping anyway. It can wait. Put it in your notes, reminders, or on your task list for later. You will just get frustrated by their lack of response because they get up at 8:30 a.m. to be at work by 8:55 a.m.

Fifth, incorporate some type of exercise. It does not have to be a lot—just something. For me, I do push-ups every day before I shower, and I take about three 2-1/2 mile walks per week. And when I take my walks, I am either in prayer or listening to a leadership podcast. Find something you enjoy, and repeat it.

Sixth, set your goals for the day. Write down whatever you want to accomplish to make that day successful. Then knock those goals out one at a time. I recommend setting no more than five goals for each day. This allows time for flexibility and the distractions that come with being in an office.

Do these six things every day for six weeks, and you will begin to master the first 120 minutes of your day. Do them for the next six months, and you will see major growth in your leadership and influence.

UNLEASH YOUR THOUGHTS

Are you waking up with purpose? How so?

_____

_____

_____

_____

_____

_____

_____

_____

_____

_____

What are your morning habits? Are they efficient and productive for your leadership?

_____

_____

_____

_____

_____

_____

_____

_____

_____

_____

Create a plan of action to begin mastering the first 120 minutes of your day.

_____

_____

_____

_____

_____

_____

_____

_____

_____

_____

_____

_____

_____

_____

_____

_____

_____

_____

_____

_____

_____

_____

_____

_____

_____

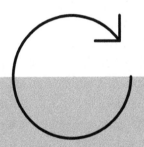

OOPS, I DID IT AGAIN

OOPS, I DID IT AGAIN

L et's talk about the F word. Failure. Nobody likes to talk about failure, but I believe failure is the womb of success. Sam Chand even edited a book about that back in 2000.[12] There is not a successful person who has ever lived on the planet who did not fail at something. Some even failed at many things! Steven Spielberg was rejected from film school three times. Henry Ford's first two car companies went under. Elvis Presley was spurned by the Grand Ole Opry and told to go back to truck driving. Failure is part of leadership!

Nobody likes to fail. That is a fact. But everybody does fail at something. There are things that leaders are going to try that will not turn out so well. Every leader has been there. Failure does not mean you are a bad leader; it just means you are a real leader. Failure is part of the job.

One year, I told our staff, "If any of you don't have at least five failures this year, you will not have a job." Now, I wasn't going to let them go, but I was challenging them to take more risks. You see, leaders have to push the envelope. We have to get to the edge of experimentation. That will often include failing in the process. John Grisham's first book, *A Time to Kill*, was rejected twenty-eight times.[13]

I have learned that failure often means you are trying something no one else has! There is no guide for it. When my wife and I started our church in 2008, we knew there was a 50/50

---

12 Sam Chand, *Failure: The Womb of Success* (Huntley, IL: Mall Publishing, 2000).

13 Emily Temple, "The Most-Rejected Books of All Time," *Literary Hub*, 5 Apr. 2019, https://lithub.com/the-most-rejected-books-of-all-time/.

chance we could fail. It was a realistic outcome for us, especially since there had not been a successful church plant like ours in over twenty years. Wow!

We look back and thank God we took a risk on failure. Now, we did not fail at our church plant, but we failed at a lot of other things we tried. We tried to be a multi-site church three times, and all three times—we failed. Did that stop us from trying? Not at all because failure is the womb of success.

Failure can be caused by a lack of planning, conflict, poor communication, absence of finances, or poor leadership decisions. But failure reveals the fact that you are trying. If you have failures on your resume, then you are a prime candidate for my team because it shows you have tried, failed, and not given up!

The saying, "Success is not final, failure is not fatal: it is the courage to continue that counts," has been attributed to many famous people. That is 100-percent true! It's really what you do after you have failed that counts. Too many people give up one failure away from a great idea or opportunity. Don't quit because you failed. Celebrate because you tried what others would not!

If you have tried something and failed, welcome to the "Oops, I Did It Again" Club.

OOPS, I DID IT AGAIN

If you have tried something and failed, welcome to the "Oops, I Did It Again" Club. Stop beating yourself up. Shake it off, and move on. Try something new. Reset and experiment again. Bill Gates said, "It's fine to celebrate success but it is more important to heed the lessons of failure."[14] What did you learn from your failure? That is the most important of all.

One year I coached my son's basketball team. It was a tough season. At the end of every game—win or lose—I would ask them, "What did you learn?" They would give me some answers. Then my response would be, "As long as we learned something, we didn't lose. We grew." You are never a failure if you grow from it!

UNLEASH YOUR THOUGHTS

Failure is part of the job. What is it about failure that scares you?

_____

_____

_____

_____

_____

_____

_____

_____

_____

_____

Where are you pushing the envelope in your leadership?

_____

_____

_____

_____

_____

_____

_____

_____

_____

_____

_____

OOPS, I DID IT AGAIN

What did you learn from your failure?

_____

_____

_____

_____

_____

_____

_____

_____

_____

_____

_____

_____

_____

_____

_____

_____

_____

_____

_____

_____

_____

_____

_____

_____

_____

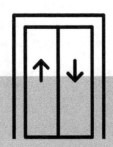

FRIENDS ARE LIKE ELEVATORS, THEY EITHER TAKE YOU UP OR THEY BRING YOU DOWN

I briefly mentioned this principle earlier, but it deserves a whole lesson because it could easily become a leader's greatest pitfall: Friends are like elevators. They either take you up, or they bring you down. My mother used to say, "Birds of a feather flock together." Basically, we are who we surround ourselves with. I know it to be true because I have seen it in my own leadership. The friends we have will determine how far we go. That's why we must choose wisely.

> *The habits of those around you will become the habits within you!*

The greatest of leaders keep their circle very tight. Jesus hung around the crowds and invested in His twelve disciples, but He spent the most time with His inner circle—Peter, James, and John. Make sure your inner circle is right and tight. It's that inner circle that's going to make you or break you as a leader.

Here's what I have learned: the habits of those around you will become the habits within you! Be very careful whom you allow to get close to you and whom you allow to speak into you. All the good, bad, and ugly that they bring will rub off on you. I am not saying, "Find perfect friends," but I am saying is find the right friends!

To be honest, I've allowed some "projects" into my inner circle, and they were always negative, always whining, always critical, and always grumbling. It got into my spirit. I found myself becoming like those individuals. They were not bad people; they were just not the right people for me. Here's the thing: as my friendship circle has gotten better, my influence has gotten larger.

At some point, every leader has to choose their elevator very carefully because it will determine how high they can go. I have this expression I adopted, "If you are not going to grow with me, you are not going to go with me." That sounds harsh but, once again, I am a New Yorker, so we either grow together, or we go in different directions. Just because your elevator is broken does not mean I have to stand in it and head nowhere.

So, what kind of people do we need in our lives? That's another million-dollar question. First, we need people who will lift our spirits. There are just some people who can make other people laugh. My kids make me laugh all the time. Yes, they can sometimes drive me crazy, but they know how to put a smile on my face. Beyond them, God has put incredible pastor-friends in my life that help lift me up when I am down and feeling discouraged.

Second, we need people who will lighten our load. We cannot surround ourselves with people who make more work for us. Get the people who give you leadership and guidance—but who also know how to lighten your load. They take things off your plate, not put more on it.

Third, we need people who will love us no matter what. No-matter-what friends are the best. I am a no-matter-what friend to my friends. If you are my friend, you've got me for life. I have had many pastor-friends who have had major moral failures take place in their lives. I will love them no matter what. I will text them, DM them, and call them. I don't care what others think. I am going to love them no matter what.

Friends are truly like elevators: they either take you up or they bring you down. Get the right friends in your circle. Start today!

UNLEASH YOUR THOUGHTS

Evaluate your circles of influence. Who needs to move closer? Who needs to move away?

_____

_____

_____

_____

_____

_____

_____

_____

_____

Do you want to be like the people who are closest to you? If not, what adjustments do you need to make?

_____

_____

_____

_____

_____

_____

_____

_____

_____

_____

FRIENDS ARE LIKE ELEVATORS, THEY EITHER TAKE YOU UP OR THEY BRING YOU DOWN

What broken elevators do you need to hop off of?

_____

_____

_____

_____

_____

_____

_____

_____

_____

_____

_____

_____

_____

_____

LESSON FORTY-FOUR

EVERY LEADER
NEEDS A LEADER

very leader needs a leader! I do not believe that people should lead without a covering. To be honest, I get a little nervous when someone has no one to answer to. That gets a little scary. Don Basham said, "Submission to spiritual authority provides the greatest spiritual protection anywhere. . . ."[15] That makes Christian leaders ones with authority but also "under authority." That does not mean our covering controls every decision we make—but they help guide us to the right decision!

> *Every leader needs a leader! No one*
> *should lead without a covering.*

Consider these verses on spiritual covering and authority:

- Hebrews 13:17—"Obey your spiritual leaders, and do what they say. Their work is to watch over your souls, and they are accountable to God. Give them reason to do this with joy and not with sorrow. That would certainly not be for your benefit."
- 1 Peter 2:13—"For the Lord's sake, submit to all human authority. . . ."
- Ephesians 4:11-12—"Now these are the gifts Christ gave to the church: the apostles, the prophets, the evangelists, and the pastors and teachers. Their

---

15 S. David Moore, *The Shepherding Movement* (New York: Bloomsbury Academic, 2004) 42.

responsibility is to equip God's people to do his work and build up the church, the body of Christ."

- 1 Thessalonians 5:12-13—"Dear brothers and sisters, honor those who are your leaders in the Lord's work. They work hard among you and give you spiritual guidance. Show them great respect and wholehearted love because of their work. And live peacefully with each other."

These verses clearly show that the church needs leadership. In fact, as you study church history—from Bible times to today—you will clearly see the need to differentiate leaders and followers. Everyone knows that anything with two heads is a monster. Imagine if every person were the leader. The natural trail of confusion would be evident. And it is. Someone has to lead, and some have to follow!

A spiritual covering involves four aspects. First, every leader needs accountability. A leader without accountability is a leader destined to fail. Being your own accountability is the recipe for a moral collapse. It does not matter what profession you are in; no one can fully hold themselves accountable. We need the right people in our lives to speak correction. Now, not everyone is called to hold you accountable. I had a gentleman in church issue me a correction after which he added, "Faithful are the wounds of a friend."

My sensitive but direct response was, "I am not your friend; I am your pastor."

Not everyone is called to hold you accountable.

Second, every leader needs trainability. The Bible calls this being teachable. When you find yourself under a covering of authority, you take the posture of "train me" because a covering is more than a title. It is about relational protection and direction. There are denominational structures that provide titles, but that does not mean they are your total spiritual covering. Yes, they provide doctrinal and behavioral correction, but they may not provide that spiritual relationship that will position you for growth. Mary and I are grateful to call Pastors David and Nicole Crank, our pastors. They invest so much time in our lives and ministry. Why? We are under their covering.

Third, every leader needs stability. A spiritual covering helps you balance your life and ministry. There is no doubt about it. Your covering will ask you the right questions, push you in the right direction, and push back when you get out of alignment. Having people over us helps keep us moving in the right direction and walking in integrity. My wife stabilizes me. My pastors stabilize me. A spiritual covering is a great stabilizer—and it helps develop longevity in ministry. Many pastors who've had moral failures had reached the point where they felt they could stabilize themselves, but they couldn't. Leaders need someone over them, or it will be over for them.

Fourth, every leader needs expandability. Our covering helps determine our potential. The more we are willing to be under someone, the more we show God what we can handle. Scripture declares, "If you are faithful in little things, you will be faithful in large ones. But if you are dishonest in little things, you won't be honest with greater responsibilities" (Luke 16:10). Faithfulness leads to fruitfulness. As you are faithful to those God has put over you, then God will expand your potential and influence!

A spiritual covering is vital in any position, but it is imperative in leadership. Without a covering, you stand unprotected. So choose your covering carefully. SPF 10 will not give you as much protection in the hot rays of the sun as SPF 50. That will provide great protection from harmful UV rays. Make sure you put on the right covering!

UNLEASH YOUR THOUGHTS

Who is your personal and ministry covering, authority, or leader (besides God and your spouse)?

_____

_____

_____

_____

_____

_____

_____

_____

_____

What's your personal accountability structure, and what improvements need to be made?

_____

_____

_____

_____

_____

_____

_____

_____

_____

When was the last time you thanked your covering? Reach out to them, and let them know how much they've impacted you!

_____

_____

_____

_____

_____

_____

_____

_____

_____

_____

_____

_____

LEAD WITH BIG-ASK FAITH

I f you were a leader in 2020, there were a lot of factors that could have shaken your faith—a global pandemic, rising interest rates, astronomical gas prices, depression, anxiety, and even loss. I get it. We all get it. But our faith is not built on the circumstances around us but on the Lord who is over us. Every leader needs big-ask faith!

> *Our faith is not built on the circumstances around us but on the Lord, who is over us. Every leader needs big-ask faith!*

Big-ask faith stands firm while the world is crumbling.
Big-ask faith remains strong when others get weak.
Big-ask faith keeps growing as soon as you start sowing.

Big-ask faith. What is this indispensable ingredient? It is defined in Hebrews 11:1: "Now faith is confidence in what we hope for and assurance about what we do not see." Basically, the writer of Hebrews is saying Faith is HOPE and VISION. It is the hope in the invisible God who gives us eyes to see! I like what Steven Furtick said: "Faith turns failure into fertilizer!" I am a preacher, and that's good. Write "Amen" in the margin right now!

I am a person of faith. I follow people of faith. I have a hard time rolling with antifaith people. It is important to surround yourself with people who are going to build you up, not bring you down.

You say, "I don't like hyperfaith people."

I hear you, but I don't like antifaith people! I'd rather live in the valley of hope than on the mountain of despair. There are more antifaith people in the world than hyperfaith people! When you say you don't like hyperfaith leaders, you are saying you can have too much faith. That's just impossible!

The Bible does not just describe faith—it prescribes it! Listen to what the Bible prescribes, "And it is impossible to please God without faith," (Hebrews 11:6). In other words, faith is a prerequisite to bringing God pleasure! Faith is required! Martin Luther King Jr. said, "Faith is taking the first step when you don't see the whole staircase," and unleashed leaders are always taking steps of big-ask faith.

Choose to be a big-ask-faith leader. If the Bible promises it, we can receive it! Don't let people talk you out of believing. Keep believing. Keep hoping. Keep trusting. Too many leaders lead without faith, but faith is a directive for spiritual leadership.

Let your big-ask faith rise higher than your doubts, larger than the haters, and bigger than you could ever imagine. This is not the time to shrink back but to advance after the calling that God has placed on your heart and life. It takes faith to lead. Check that—it takes big-ask faith to lead.

Let them call you crazy! Let them believe you've lost it! They didn't create your destiny, and they cannot cancel it. Who are "they" anyway? Your faith, as a Christian leader, will set you apart from any other leader on the planet. Here's why! Big-ask faith takes the pressure off of you because you are putting your trust in God. And leaders who lead without pressure are more likely to lead with higher purpose and greater passion.

Get your faith up! If God promised it, He will accomplish it. Trust Him in the process. Just because you are surrounded by a culture without faith doesn't mean you can't still choose to lead with big-ask faith!

UNLEASH YOUR THOUGHTS

Write down 2 to 3 specific things you need big-ask faith for!

_____

_____

_____

_____

_____

_____

_____

_____

_____

_____

_____

_____

_____

_____

_____

_____

_____

_____

_____

_____

_____

_____

_____

_____

What failures that are currently holding you back do you need God to turn into fertilizer for your future?

_____

_____

_____

_____

_____

_____

_____

_____

_____

_____

_____

_____

_____

Have you truly been living with biblical faith? Grow your faith today!

_____

_____

_____

_____

_____

_____

_____

_____

IF YOU DON'T SET YOUR PRIORITIES SOMEONE ELSE WILL

Did you know that priority management is more important than time management? Oh, yes, it is! If you don't set your priorities, your time management is a waste of effort because you will make good time but have no purpose attached to your life.

> *If you don't set your priorities, your time management is a waste of effort because you will make good time but have no purpose attached to your life.*

Priorities are about making pre-decisions—making a decision about what matters before you have to make a decision. Set your priorities from out of the leadership gate. As you set your priorities, they will make your schedule, decisions, calendar, and staffing easier.

For me, I have a priority to build the church of Jesus until the day I die. My life, leadership, schedule, and purpose all revolve around that priority. That single priority sets an order for the rest of them. My family is also part of that priority. I get to build with them, but I also have the honor to do life with my bride and children. Not everyone reading this is a pastor, so your priority may be slightly different. If you are a Christian, our priority will be the same. Our duty is to continue to do what Jesus started.

There are four general priorities every leader must develop in order to unleash their destiny. First, our priority must be set on eternity. The number one function of leadership in the life of a Christian is to impact people's eternities. It's really that simple. Every Christian leader must view every decision and discussion through the lens of eternity. How will this shape someone's life forever?

Second, our priority should be to cultivate unique callings. We all have a general purpose, but God has also given each person a specific reason for being. Everything that you put in your schedule should help cultivate your calling and the calling of those you get to lead. Sometimes you will have to say no to good things, so you can say yes to your calling.

Third, our priority should be the first thought—not the last response—of our team. Your team has to know your calling. If they don't, they will try and distract you every single time from walking in it. Remember that your team's primary function is not to determine who you are, what you do, or how you lead. That's your job for them. Your team or staff must come alongside you to help you fulfill your God-given potential.

Fourth, our priority must be to invest in those we lead. Whether we are part of a business, church, or nonprofit, God has put us in the position we are in not just for our own growth but to grow those around us. I do weekly staff meetings with the entire team. We hit some housecleaning items, but I spend about forty-five minutes or more teaching our team leadership tools to put in their toolbox. They may not need them now, but at some point, they will. The pace of change is speeding up, but that should not affect your priorities. Your priorities are not impacted or impaired by the environment around you but the pre-decisions you made before you had to. Remember, if you don't set your priorities, someone else will. Now, go and write down what matters to you, and shout it from the rooftop!

UNLEASH YOUR THOUGHTS

How much time do you spend setting your priorities: daily, weekly, monthly, or yearly?

_____

_____

_____

_____

_____

_____

Reevaluate your current priorities. What needs to shift down? What needs to move up? What needs to come off your list? What needs to be added?

_____

_____

_____

_____

_____

_____

_____

_____

_____

_____

_____

_____

_____
_____
_____
_____
_____
_____

How can you better guard your priorities?

_____
_____
_____
_____
_____
_____
_____
_____
_____
_____
_____
_____
_____
_____
_____
_____
_____
_____
_____
_____

WHEN SOMEONE SHOWS YOU WHO THEY ARE BELIEVE THEM

I have made the mistake many times of thinking I can fix somebody. Part of my problem is that I see someone's potential and often overlook their red flags. Have you ever done that? Too often, I break my own advice, but when I do, I find myself back to "When someone shows you who they are, believe them."

If someone you are dating cheats on you, then believe they will probably cheat on you when you're married. If someone lies to you about the little things, trust me; they will lie to you about the big things. If any employee is a great interviewee, then there is a high probability they have been in a lot of interviews (usually, these people can't hold jobs). What am I trying to say? People will show you who they are all the time, and when they do, believe them.

> *People will show you who they are all the time, and when they do, believe them.*

"You are a pastor," you say, "don't you believe people can change?" Of course, I do. I see life-change every day. But people will never just change for you; they typically change for themselves first! That's why when someone reveals who they are, you have to ask yourself, *Do I have the time to invest in this person's growth?* If you do not, then do not bring them close to you. You'll get frustrated, and so will they.

I have another confession: I don't hire projects. What I mean is that I am not going to hire someone who has character or competency flaws that I identify in the interview process. If they can't hide them in an interview, the job will further expose them. Don't hire by pity; hire by purpose.

Now, most people stay on the negative side, but let's shift over to the positive side of this lesson. As your team begins to grow and achieve all that God has designed them for, celebrate it. Sometimes leaders have an easy time seeing the negative but find it hard to celebrate the positive. If someone is consistently on time, don't think they are going to start coming late. Or, if someone proves that they can be trusted, don't start doubting them because of your insecurity.

People truly are good. Not all, but the vast majority of people, employees, and leaders desire to do the right thing. See the good and celebrate it. As your team demonstrates their ability to be trusted, don't allow past experiences to destroy current relationships. That is a huge struggle for most leaders. They see everyone through the lens of someone else. That's not fair to that person. See each person as an individual. When they prove their worth, believe them!

Here's a huge principle for leaders today: not everyone is out to get you. Ouch! I know that is tough to read, but it is very true. However, we allow past experiences to distort current realities. Your team wants you to succeed—that's why they serve your vision. And when they don't, they find another job.

If someone is on your team, they most likely want to be there. They are showing loyalty.

Dealing with personalities is challenging but not impossible. As people show us who they are, our job is to help them become a better version of themselves. Don't cut someone off just because they have some areas that need refining. Our job, as leaders, is to help people grow to the next level as they show us who they are. But just know, people will always reveal more than they can conceal. The real person always floats to the surface.

UNLEASH YOUR THOUGHTS

Have you overlooked red flags lately just to try and salvage a relationship or not to hurt someone's feelings? How do you need to address that situation?

_____

_____

_____

_____

_____

_____

_____

_____

_____

_____

_____

_____

_____

_____

Who do you show people you are?

_____

_____

_____

_____

_____

_____

_____

_____

_____

_____

Which side of this equation do you tend to fall on—the positive or the negative? How can you be more intentional about recognizing and discerning people from the other side?

_____

_____

_____

_____

_____

_____

_____

_____

_____

_____

_____

_____

_____

_____

_____

THE ART OF
THE PIVOT

One of the most important keys to life and leadership is being able to pivot. Over the years, I have discovered that the best leaders are those who can adjust quickly or change rapidly. Dictionary.com describes a pivot as "a pin, point, or short shaft on the end of which something rests and turns, or upon and about which something rotates or oscillates." Every leader needs a good pivot.

> Over the years, I have discovered that the best leaders are those who can adjust quickly or change rapidly.

The key elements of a successful pivot are as follows.: P(riorities) I(ntercession), V(ision), O(bedience), and T(iming). Let me break them down for you.

PRIORITIES—Don't let a good opportunity overwhelm your God opportunities. That is based on priorities. Any pivot that takes you off your God-given priorities is probably an adjustment you should not make or take. That's why every leader must establish their priorities early. Never let anyone or anything hijack your life. Stay focused on your priorities.

INTERCESSION—Pray. Pray. Pray. If you get an opportunity presented to you, it is imperative to bathe it in prayer. It is great to get advice, but making sure that God is in it is even more important. We have this expression we say all the time at our church: "Pray it to life." In other words, if God has called us to it, no matter what, He will bring us through it! Talk to God. Get His consent above anyone else's.

VISION—Does this line up with your vision? Just because something is put in your lap does not mean you should take it in your hands. Sometimes you have to give opportunities back because they do not line up with your vision. Pastor David Crank says, "If it's God today, it'll be God tomorrow." That means you don't have to change your vision every time the wind blows. Be consistent. Stay true to the vision God has called you to. If it violates your vision, it may not be the right pivot.

OBEDIENCE—At some point, you just have to obey when God speaks. When God calls you to make an adjustment or to take advantage of a moment, you have to just do it. You see, knowing God's will is a lot easier than obeying it. If God tells you to start a church, launch a business, or go on a mission trip, you will eventually have to obey. So, when God tells you to pivot your responsibility, just obey.

TIMING—And, yes, some pivots aren't immediate. The timing has to be right. The Bible says there is a time for everything. And that means you have to make sure you are in the right season for a major adjustment. In John C. Maxwell's *The 21 Irrefutable Laws of Leadership*, Law 19 has to do with timing. It essentially says the wrong thing at the wrong time is the wrong thing. The right thing at the wrong time is still the wrong thing. But the right thing at the right time is the right thing. Timing matters.

THE ART OF THE PIVOT

Every single person and leader I know of who excels has mastered the art of the pivot. Put every adjustment or change through the above five filters, and I believe it will save you a lot of heartache and heartbreak! Now, get out there and ask God, "Where do I need a good pivot?"

UNLEASH YOUR THOUGHTS

Recall a time when you pivoted away from what God wanted you to do. What lessons have you learned or can you learn from that time?

_____

_____

_____

_____

_____

_____

_____

_____

_____

_____

_____

_____

Honest assessment: How do you feel you are with change and adaptation? Where and how can you improve?

_____

_____

_____

_____

_____

_____

_____

_____

_____

_____

_____

_____

_____

_____

_____

_____

_____

_____

What pivot are you wrestling with right now that you know you just need to obey?

_____

_____

_____

_____

_____

_____

_____

_____

_____

_____

_____

_____

_____

NEVER FORGET WHERE YOU STARTED

After the home-going of my mom, I made the trip to her celebration service with my two daughters. (My son had COVID-19 at the time—so he and my wife stayed home). Before the service for my mom, I decided to take my girls down memory lane. In fact, I started at the first church I ever worked—Redeeming Love Fellowship in Hartford, New York.

It was a small upstate New York church with about fifteen members when I first arrived there. I wish I could say it was a great experience. It was not. That's why it only lasted nine months. It is one of the only things I have ever quit in my life. (The other was McDonald's after a three or four hour shift.) It was not the sexiest way to jump into ministry. To be honest, after that nine months, I was ready to throw in the towel.

I learned a lesson early in life, though: leaders don't quit; they pivot. It was in that dark place that I first learned the art of the pivot. What is that? The art of the pivot is simply finding another way when things don't go your way. Leaders don't quit; they pivot. I had to learn really quickly how to pivot, and I have been pivoting ever since.

> *Sometimes the only way to get ahead is to look behind—to see how far you have come.*

Never forget where you started. It keeps you humble and hungry. I am so grateful for a rough start in ministry because it taught me to appreciate every single thing that

I experience—good or bad. Sometimes the only way to get ahead is to look behind—to see how far you have come. It has been miraculous to see God's hand on this little boy from Buffalo, New York.

My mom passed away on November 1, 2021. She had written all of her boys a note that we saw only after she passed away. I will cherish the entire paragraph of wisdom she unloaded on me, but one line will continue to challenge me to walk in my calling: "Continue to walk in the anointing of the Lord and God will use you in a great and mighty way." Dang. That line had been written seven years previously, but it was for me. It was a reminder to stay true to the purpose for which God placed me on the planet.

Sometimes you have to look behind in order to get ahead. Learn from the past, but don't live in the past. Rewind into your history to get a glimpse of how far you have come. The highs and lows are all part of your story. They have made you who you are today!

Never forget your humble beginnings because they allow you to celebrate your current blessings. Never forget where you started, but don't stay stuck there. Keep moving. Keep grinding.

Remember where you began. Your first job. Your first book deal. Your first pain. Your first company. Your first heartbreak. Your first opportunity. Remember the firsts!

Every leader who has ever been unleashed to make a difference has looked back on where they began. How we grow up shapes who we are! That's why looking back is vital to the emotional health of every leader. If your boss is acting like a bully, then maybe they were bullied as a child. If your employee always needs praise, then maybe it's because they didn't get celebrated as a child. Where you began helps determine who you are and how far you can go. Never forget where you started!

UNLEASH YOUR THOUGHTS

When was the last time you thanked God for where you started? Thank Him, and tell Him why you're thankful!

_____

_____

_____

_____

_____

_____

_____

_____

What can you learn from the story of your beginning?

_____

_____

_____

_____

_____

_____

_____

_____

_____

_____

_____

NEVER FORGET WHERE YOU STARTED

When was the last time you celebrated how far you've come? What are some milestones you can celebrate today?

_____

_____

_____

_____

_____

_____

_____

_____

_____

_____

_____

_____

_____

_____

_____

_____

_____

WHAT YOU MAKE HAPPEN FOR OTHERS GOD WILL MAKE HAPPEN FOR YOU

About twelve years ago, Mary and I had the privilege of being introduced to Joel Osteen. It was a small, intimate gathering of about twelve pastors/leaders. It was an incredible moment for us. We could never imagine in our wildest dreams how that one moment would catapult our destiny. We have come to respect Pastors Joel and Victoria so much as we have seen their love for God, people, and pastors. It is infectious.

Someone once said, "You can be a big part of a small thing, or you can be a small part of a big thing." We are so honored to cheer on Joel and Victoria. They are true champions.

Several years later, I took my son, Malachi, with me to one of Pastor Joel's book signings on Long Island. I go every time, but this was the first time I took Malachi. We gave out over six hundred invites to Church Unleashed. It was a great moment. After the signing, we went into the back room with Pastor Joel. He was so gracious (as he always is). First thing he asked was, "How are you doing? How is the church?" Over all our years of friendship, I have learned that Pastor Joel is always concerned about YOU. That's not even debatable. He always asks, "How are *you* doing? How's the church? How is the family?"

I mentioned, "I will see you at TBN tomorrow. Excited to see you and Joseph Prince. I would love to meet him one day."

Pastor Joel said, "Remind me."

Johnny (Joel's armor bearer) handed me his cell phone and said, "Put your number in there."

I did. I could never have imagined what would happen next. It's crazy what God does!

I went to the TBN show in NYC—as I'd planned beforehand—but I never thought that Pastor Joel would remember; he has so much on his plate. Johnny motioned to me and took me to the greenroom to see Joel—who then introduced me to Joseph Prince. What? Pinch me. Crazy moment.

Emotions rose as I stood there with my friend Joel Osteen and new friend Joseph Prince. I could not believe it. It still gets to me. Pastor Joel took time to make something happen for me. He did not have to. He wanted to. Wow! The doors that God has opened up for this little boy from Buffalo, New York, blow my mind.

I believe humility is the key to success. People often ask me, "Todd, what makes Joel Osteen different?" I can honestly tell you that it is HUMILITY. Mary and I have never met anyone as humble as him. There is no greater quality that God can use. Scripture declares, "Humble yourselves before God . . . he will lift you up" (James 4:10). God has used Pastors Joel and Victoria because they remain humble.

I pray that as you remain a humble leader, God will open up some incredible doors for you, but never forget those doors can quickly close if pride swells up.

I also know that honor starts at the top. I have never been part of something that bleeds as much honor as Lakewood Church. Every pastor, staff member, leader, and volunteer serves with honor. They are kind, caring, and committed to all people. It is an amazing thing to see. But that all starts at the top. Pastors Joel and Victoria live and lead with honor. There is not a person they don't try to honor. That's why Pastor Joel will spend three hours at a book signing. He makes sure he signs every person's book.

It's like Dr. Seuss's *Oh, the Places You'll Go*. Mary and I stand amazed. Never in our wildest dreams did we ever believe God could use us the way He is, open up the doors He has, or have us cross paths with the people He has. It is all His doing. We could not be where we are, do what we do, or know who we know without JESUS. I can't wait to see what God has in store for us next.

> *Do unto others—not as you would have them do to you—but what has already been done for you!*

I pray that you, as a leader, will make happen for others what others have made happen for you. Do unto others—not as you would have them do to you—but what has already been done for you! Find someone to elevate! Take time to invest in someone—with no hope of anything in return—and I know God will open doors for your life that you could never imagine. Our family is living proof.

UNLEASH YOUR THOUGHTS

What opportunities did you receive because someone else made them happen for you?

_____

_____

_____

_____

_____

_____

_____

_____

_____

_____

_____

_____

_____

Are any of those opportunities ones that you can now, in turn, make happen for anyone else?

_____

_____

_____

_____

_____

_____

_____

_____

_____

_____

_____

_____

_____

_____

_____

How have you seen this principle play out in your life to date?

_____

_____

_____

_____

_____

_____

_____

_____

_____

_____

_____

_____

_____

_____

HONOR. HONOR. HONOR.

I believe in the principle of honor. A friend of mine, Joseph Nieves, reminds me often, "Honor is the currency of heaven." Author Gene Herndon, writes in his book *The Eyes of Honor*, "Honor has become a lost art in today's society. We see dishonor not only in the world but unfortunately in the church."[16] He then goes on to say that honor "becomes the vehicle by which blessing flows."

> *Here's what I have learned about honor: everyone wants it, but few know how to give it.*

Here's what I have learned about honor: everyone wants it, but few know how to give it. We talk of honor, but do we know how to lead in it. That's why one of our "Unleashed Codes" (values that drive our church) is that we exist to create a culture of honor. It's about honoring up—honoring those above us. It's about honoring down—those we lead. It's about honoring all around—extending honor to every person. We have to fight for this culture every day.

Honor is critical to the success of your business or organization—no matter how large or small. That's why it is something we make part of our culture. Our organization does that by elevating, encouraging, and empowering people. Those three things are what we do on a regular basis to make sure honor is evident in every aspect of our work.

---

16 Gene Herndon, *The Eyes of Honor* (Glendale, AZ: Aion Multimedia, 2019).

I read somewhere recently that dishonor equals dysfunction. Oh, dang! That's red-hot good. When you find employees dishonoring their bosses, you have dysfunction, but you also have it when employers are dishonoring their employees. Honor is a two-way street.

Let me give you a few signs of dishonor in the workplace:

- A negative attitude.
- Neglecting your job or not finishing your tasks.
- Ignoring other employees.
- Poorly timed sarcasm (may be for NYers only).
- Not being coachable or teachable.
- Always having an answer before someone finishes.
- Not receiving criticism from your manager.
- Talking down to people.
- Playing the victim to get out of trouble.
- Coming in late or leaving early.

I believe that honor begins at the top. It is the responsibility of top-level leaders to demonstrate honor at the highest level. If you, as a leader, cannot demonstrate honor, then you cannot expect your team to build a culture of honor. It all starts with you.

First Peter 2:17 (NIV) reads, "Show proper respect to everyone." It is the job of every leader to respect those who serve alongside you in accomplishing the vision and mission that God has put you on planet Earth for. When you honor others, they will honor you. If they don't, keep showing them honor. You are not responsible for their lack of honor, but you are definitely responsible for yours!

HONOR. HONOR. HONOR.

Honor. Period. It's something we need to fight for every single day. The moment you lose your culture of honor is the moment you lose the capacity to do what your organization exists for.

Honor those whom you agree with and disagree with. Honor those who look like you and those that do not. Honor those who have more than you and those that have less. Simply put, honor everyone—all the time, every time.

UNLEASH YOUR THOUGHTS

What's your honor quotient? Do you live a life of intentional honor?

_____

_____

_____

_____

_____

_____

_____

_____

_____

_____

Do you give honor more than you seek it?

_____

_____

_____

_____

_____

_____

_____

_____

_____

Who are the hardest people in your life to honor? The easiest? Why?

_____

_____

_____

_____

_____

_____

_____

_____

_____

_____

_____

_____

_____

_____

_____

_____

_____

_____

_____

_____

_____

_____

_____

LEAD LIKE IT'S THE FIRST AND LAST DAY OF YOUR LIFE

L eadership is a gift. It's a gift that we value and treasure. Therefore, it's a gift that we must protect. That's why I believe we have to lead like it's the first and last day of our lives. The first day, so you remain excited about every opportunity. The last day, so you leave it all on the field after every opportunity. Too many leaders lose their edge because they have lost their passion.

> *We have to lead like it's the first and last day of our lives.*

Serving in various capacities and places of leadership over nearly three decades has been filled with challenges. That is without doubt, but I have never lost my passion or drive to lead. In fact, I believe I am more determined today than I may have ever been. One day, when God calls this leader home to heaven, I pray I will be able to say, "I gave it everything I had. I was faithful to my wife, led my family, invested in my children, and honored you, oh, God, with my leadership." And then I will hear these words from Jesus, "Well done, good and faithful servant" (Matthew 25:23). Notice two things in this short statement. The first is well done. It does not say "well thought" or "well imagined." No, it says, "Well done." That means I have to do something with the gifts, talents, and abilities God has blessed me with. I want to do it with all my heart and with excellence.

Also, we are to be servants. I am called to do what my Master tells me to do. I am God's servant-leader. Leaders must be willing to stoop down into the manure if that's what they are asked to do. At the end of my leadership journey, the only title I want to hear from Jesus is, "Todd, you were a good and faithful servant." So I lead like it's the first and last day of my life!

Leadership is tough. In fact, some days, leadership sucks. That is a harsh reality. When you have to let someone go or give correction to a staff member, those things are never easy, but they are part of leadership. Enjoy the journey!

Have you ever had first-day jitters? Do you remember the excitement you felt when you first started leading? Have you lost it? It's time to get it back again. Leadership has its highs and lows, but I promise you that if you can keep your purpose, you will never lose your passion. Most people lose their way because they lost their why. Get your why back! Look back, and rediscover why you started that business, opened that church, or launched that nonprofit. Find that joy again. If you can't find it, fake it until the joy shows up! If you stay in the game of leadership long enough, you'll find that place of peace again.

What about last-day hope? Oh, yes, all of us will finish our leadership journey. It's never an if but always a when. The Bible teaches us about this concept called stewardship. In other words, be faithful with what you have. Faithfulness is not a celebrated leadership trait on earth, but in heaven, it is the most valuable. Jesus taught this principle when He said, "But the one who endures to the end will be saved" (Matthew 24:13). Faithfulness, endurance, and perseverance are the eternal qualities of a leader that God will reward. Be faithful. Remain consistent.

God sees all that you do. Even the things no one else sees: late nights, early mornings. . . . Be faithful, and I promise you will become fruitful! Choose to lead each day like it is the first and last day of your life. You will live differently. You will love differently. You will lead differently.

UNLEASH YOUR THOUGHTS

Are you currently leading with more passion than ever before?

_____

_____

_____

Do you remember why you started? Sit down, and write out your why.

_____

_____

_____

_____

_____

_____

_____

_____

_____

_____

_____

_____

_____

_____

_____

_____

Is there anything in the way of you leading with "first and last day" energy and excitement? If so, how can you remove those things?

_____

_____

_____

_____

_____

_____

_____

_____

_____

_____

_____

_____

_____

_____

_____

_____

_____

_____

_____

_____

_____

_____

_____

_____

CLOSING THOUGHTS

Wow, you did it! You read all fifty-two *Leadership Unleashed* lessons. I am so honored that you took time to grow your leadership. I pray that God unleashes the leader on the inside of your ministry, your job, your family, and your life. This journey of leadership is a marathon, not a sprint. Enjoy the journey, and watch how God helps you develop your gifts, talents, and abilities.

Let me say this: leadership is not easy. It is full of challenges and difficulties that test our faith, trust, and will. My friend Paul Bartholomew used to always say, "Leaders can't serve with a glass jaw," As I wrote in chapter 8. In other words, at some point, it's just your job to suck it up and take it on the chin. That's not unfair—it's just leadership. Let me write that again. That's not unfair—that's just leadership.

We face highs and lows on a daily basis, but the need for real leadership in our world today is at an all-time high. So, whether you serve in the boardroom, sanctuary, cafe, or home, God has uniquely called and qualified you to lead where you are. Remember, no one can beat you at being you. So, just be you, and watch how your leadership is unleashed into another stratosphere of influence. You see, your home, school, and/or workplace needs to see real leadership in operation. You have a gift and a responsibility.

There is not a single book that can supernaturally inspire your leadership, not even this one, except for the Bible. I believe that the Bible is the greatest leadership book that has ever been written. Yes, it's about God. Yes, it's about Jesus. Yes, it's a religious book. But that single book has revolutionized the world in ways no other leadership book has. If, as John C. Maxwell says, "Leadership is truly influence, nothing more, nothing less," then the Bible is the greatest book on leadership ever written.

Let me issue you a challenge—read the Bible!

"I am not religious."

That's okay! Just read it, and look for leadership principles and pitfalls. As you read the most purchased and read book of all time, you will discover things about your life and leadership that will help unleash it. It's a challenge, and every leader rises to a challenge.

I would love to hear from you. Seriously, I would love your feedback and learnings from *LEADERSHIP UNLEASHED*.

So, follow me on social media @toddrbishop or email me at todd@toddbishop.tv. It would be my honor to continue the conversation because great leaders don't grow alone. They grow together!

Again, thank you for investing in yourself. Now, go out, and unleash your leadership!

Drive the principles of this book home and take your team to the next level by purchasing the **Unleash Your Team** *Group Study Guide!*

UNLEASHED LIFE PRAYER

Father, I believe and declare that you will **unleash my life and leadership.** There is nothing that hell throws at me that can keep me from accomplishing my purpose. I am protected, secured, empowered, anointed, equipped, and well-able to become everything You designed me to be.

I believe and declare that my past is forgiven, my present is redeemed, and my future is secure. Every thing that my hand touches turns to gold, and every place I put my foot becomes my inheritance. I am walking in favor, living in blessing, and embracing abundance. **I am living the unleashed life**.

I believe and declare that God is directing my steps, opening the right doors, and taking me places I could never take myself. I am blessed coming in and blessed going out. I am first and never last. I am above and never beneath. I am an heir of all that God has. So, no matter what I experience I will always excel as God **unleashes my life** in ways I could never imagine.

I believe and declare I will be blessed, favored, equipped, and empowered to live **the unleashed life**. I will stay planted in God's Word and my life will flourish.

I believe and declare that the rest of my life will be the best of my life. Father, I ask you to **unleash** everything I need to become everything you designed me to be. In Jesus' name, Amen.

UNLEASHED
NETWORK

JOIN THE NETWORK BY PASTORS FOR PASTORS

Our goal is to embrace, equip, and empower the local church to become everything it is designed to be. Together we create opportunities to grow leaders and grow churches!

BENEFITS

CONNECTION
Build relationships with like-minded pastors and church leaders.

CONTENT
Access to a variety of downloadable resources & content.

CONFERENCES
Attend conferences, labs, & roundtables for no cost.

COACHING
Access to one-on-one, individualized consulting at significant discount.

CONTACT

 MYA@TODDBISHOP.TV   WWW.TODDBISHOP.TV   @UNLEASHED_NETWORK

YOU DON'T GO TO THE NEXT LEVEL - YOU GROW TO THE NEXT LEVEL!

LIFE COACHING WITH TODD BISHOP

OUR MISSION
TO UNLEASH THE LEADER ON THE INSIDE OF YOU

OUR VALUES

TEAMWORK   EXCELLENCE   INTEGRITY   CREATIVITY   SIMPLICITY

If you have any questions please contact us at
mya@toddbishop.tv